The Real Deal
Danny Dyer

The Real Deal
Danny Dyer

The unauthorised biography of Britain's toughest star

Martin Howden

JOHN BLAKE

Published by John Blake Publishing Ltd,
3 Bramber Court, 2 Bramber Road,
London W14 9PB, England

www.johnblakepublishing.co.uk

First published in paperback in 2010

ISBN: 9781843581802

British Library Cataloguing-in-Publication Data:

A catalogue record for this book is available from the British Library.

Design by www.envydesign.co.uk

Printed in Great Britain by CPI Bookmarque Ltd, Croydon

3 5 7 9 10 8 6 4 2

Papers used by John Blake Publishing are natural, recyclable products
made from wood grown in sustainable forests. The manufacturing processes
conform to the environmental regulations of the country of origin.

Contents

Chapter One	The East-End Kid	1
Chapter Two	Dyer Straits	9
Chapter Three	A Prime Talent	19
Chapter Four	An Actor's Life for Me	29
Chapter Five	Stopping Traffic	37
Chapter Six	Give Danny a Supporting Hand	51
Chapter Seven	In the Spotlight	65
Chapter Eight	It's a Funny Old Game	75
Chapter Nine	A Tough Love	95
Chapter Ten	Childhood Sweetheart	103
Chapter Eleven	Danny's World Cup Adventure	111
Chapter Twelve	Controversy in Cannes	125
Chapter Thirteen	The Holiday of a Lifetime	133
Chapter Fourteen	Back in Business	151
Chapter Fifteen	Danny and Friends	157
Chapter Sixteen	Laughing his Head Off	169

Chapter Seventeen	Danny's Dyer-bolical Mouth	189
Chapter Eighteen	Outlaw	195
Chapter Nineteen	Danny and the Sex-Files	213
Chapter Twenty	Going to America	223
Chapter Twenty-One	A New Stage in Danny's Life	231
Chapter Twenty-Two	Danny on the Telly	237
Chapter Twenty-Three	Danny the Family Man	251
Chapter Twenty-Four	The Future's not Dyer for Danny	257
Chapter Twenty-Five	A Difficult Year for Danny	260

Chapter One

The East-End Kid

I'm just a peasant from East London

If you were walking down the streets of Britain during the hot summer of 1977 you would find it hard to ignore the nation's fascination with a little sci-fi film known as *Star Wars*. Shot on a shoestring budget and little favoured by its own studio Twentieth Century-Fox to do much business, it went on to become a box-office behemoth, with a generation of children transfixed by the dazzling special effects and ageless story of good vs evil.

Long queues snaked around corners packed with curious cinemagoers either eager to see what the fuss was about or reliving the experience for the second, third or fourth time, or even into double figures.

And there was, of course, the sight of kids nursing grazed knees while trying to get to grips with a new outdoor pastime called the skateboard, or teenagers proudly wearing disco jump suits or – the ubiquitous sight of the 1970s – flares.

But who cares that the country was in the throes of Hollywood fever or the imported fashion and hobbies? This is the story of a British boy who is inextricably linked to his country of birth. In fact, his city of birth to be more precise.

London, in 1977, was having its moment in the sun – and, quite rightly, there would be things that would interest Danny more than wielding a lightsabre.

The longest-running current-affairs programme in the world, *Panorama*, turned its eyes on the violent and unsavoury phenomenon of football hooligans in 1997 – the Millwall firm in particular. It was the first time that the violent pastime was explored fully on TV and it shocked the watching nation. It is generally believed that football hooliganism started in the late 1960s and peaked in the 1970s and 1980s before the Heysel and Hillsborough disasters forced England to clean up their game. However, a certain film in 2004 would ensure that the topic would rear its head again.

If London didn't have enough to contend with, what with the bone-crunching violence on the football terraces, the city was also in the clutches of a thrashing, noisy and rebellious sound called punk music, which exploded in 1977, with the release of seminal records *Never Mind The Bollocks Here Comes The Sex Pistols* and The Clash's self-titled debut. The Clash's song '1977' had lyrics sneering 'No Elvis, Beatles or the Rolling Stones', while tabloid tales were awash with stories of spitting, bloody noses and broken bones at punk gigs in the capital. The *Daily Mirror* famously dubbed the scene as 'THE FILTH AND THE FURY'.

While football hooliganism was to play a huge part in Danny's career, punk music could have had its part too. The actor claims he was set to play The Sex Pistols' Sid Vicious in an explosive biopic of the late rocker. Hugely respected indie actress Chloë Sevigny was lined up to play Nancy and it was to be shot in San Francisco in 2000. It would have been a dream come true for Danny because, not only was he a huge Sex Pistols fan, he also knew exactly how he wanted to play the punk rocker. 'I'd like to play Sid Vicious, my ideal role,' he said on his official website. 'There's only been one other film about The Sex Pistols, *Sid and Nancy*. Gary Oldman, who's one of my idols, played him in a way I would have done differently. There was so much to him. This was a geezer who couldn't play guitar, a raving lunatic. But he was an icon and there was a reason for that, you know, the charisma.' Unfortunately, an actor's strike a week before production wrecked that dream. 'I was devastated,' he admits. He concedes that he's probably too old to play him now.

Punk represented a London that was unhappy with its current Parliament leadership and spiralling unemployment. The Sex Pistols' safety pins clasping tattered clothes attire has more than once been interpreted as a visual reminder of the unemployment rate.

Custom House, Canning Town, in East London was one of many places in Britain bearing the brunt of the times. Situated in the London Borough of Newham and in the former docks on the north side of the River Thames, Canning Town is a multi-cultural community – one that established an African mariner population in the early

20th century thanks to shipping links between West Africa and the Caribbean. While it remains in the top five per cent of the most deprived areas in London, Canning Town is currently undergoing a nearly £2 billion regeneration project.

But on 24 July 1977, at Plaistow's Maternity Hospital, to the joy of Anthony and Christiana Joyce Dyer, Daniel John Dyer was born in Newham – a place which he has described as a 'shit hole, a real fucking concrete jungle'.

'I was brought up in that environment – quite homophobic, quite racist, very set in their ways. It's changing a lot now obviously. The Olympics are supposed to make it glamorous but they're forgetting about the crack heads. But as a youngster that is what I was brought up with.'

His Woodside Community School classmate Lindsay Hamilton agreed, calling the area that they both come from a 'tough place'. Despite having 'fuck all. We never had any money or anything like that', or perhaps because of it, Danny's house was a loving one. His fiancée Joanne Mas has described Danny as the affectionate one in their relationship, which is something that has come from his family. 'My family is not short of a cuddle. There's a lot of love there,' he once said.

And it starts from the top down, beginning with the formidable Nana Polly. A proper matriarch, she ruled the family with a loving fist. Danny loves a strong woman (as displayed by his relationship with his partner Joanne) and that is down to his beloved Nana. She is someone he desperately looks up to, and is someone who was a rock of support when his parents split up when he was nine. He has constantly credited Polly as being a strong influence when he was growing up. Talking about his relationship with women in a 2007 *Observer* article, he said, 'Everything I know about women I learned from my nan. I went to live with her and my granddad at an early age when my parents split up. She was a good influence on me. She's a very strong woman and doesn't take nonsense from anyone.'

While he hails Polly for her stabling influence, he can also thank her for acquiring one of his most distinctive habits – his foul mouth, and the c-word in particular.

'Nana Polly swears every other sentence. My mother says it but she has to have a reason. My nan says it whenever she sees Stephen Hendry [snooker player] on the telly. "I can't stand that cunt, cunt, cunt... How's them potatoes, cunt?" It's a normal way of life.'

It's clear he has an incredibly close relationship with his grandmother, and one that still remains to this day. 'My nan's still running about in East London though, in her Reebok Classics, up at 4.30am every day for work, at seventy-eight. She's very old school. She cooks me ox heart. Just a heart on a plate with a few Brussels sprouts around it.'

While he 'loved those days' with his nan, it was, of course, a huge personal turmoil as it is for any child coming to terms with a broken family home. Unfortunately, Danny also had another personal trauma round the corner. His granddad – Polly's husband – was dying from cancer. He was diagnosed with cancer not long after Danny moved in with his grandparents. Rather than being shielded from it, Danny rolled his sleeves up and helped to take care of him until his death. Unsurprisingly, his death hit Danny extremely hard. 'My granddad got cancer not long after I moved in and I helped look after him. When he died I stayed. It was devastating when he went because I never thought he would,' he remembers. 'He was a big man, he was in the navy, and then he deteriorated in front of my eyes.'

The double blow of losing his granddad and the day-to-day attention of his dad shaped the young Danny's childhood and early teenage years. He admits that because of the split he 'didn't have much discipline'.

His upbringing in Plaistow's Holborn Road was one that you would typify with a working-class family. 'Everyone's set in their ways, woman stays at home, dad goes to work, dad has a beer every night, mother stays in with the kids,' he recalled.

Danny's dad is, according to director Nick Love, 'a fucking colossus. Proper old school, out the flats, works at a building site and all that. Drinks fully pasteurised milk and everything. Top man. He's got pictures of Satan tattoos and all that.'

Anthony Dyer was a painter and decorator by trade. A loving and affectionate man, he instilled proper old-fashioned values in Danny – not only in life but also in a sense of pride in where he comes from. He would take Danny to see his beloved West Ham United at Upton Park. The team, and football in general, would be something that would for ever be attributed to Danny's image, as would football hooliganism, which would be prevalent at London football grounds in those days. 'As a kid, being a stand away, safe with my dad, it was an amazing thing,' he recalled. 'What on earth is going on? Why are these men doing this to each other?' However, going to the football was something he would love and would repeat long into his adult life. Speaking in 2007, he said, 'My favourite walk is from my house to Upton Park, West Ham's ground. I love walking along with all the other fans, experiencing the excitement of match day and grabbing a burger and a couple of beers on the way.'

As well as regular Saturdays watching his cherished Hammers, his parents would take him on annual trips to Canvey Island. The seaside resort, which was a popular holiday destination for thousands of Londoners before tourism declined in the late 1970s and early 1980s, is an island lying seven miles off the southern coast of Essex in the Thames Estuary.

Danny would wait impatiently in the car, it seemingly taking ages to get to this magical place full of rides and candyfloss. One of his earliest memories was heading to Canvey Island when he was two-and-a-half years old. 'My dad used to take us every year, and at the time I thought it was Disney World, but it really wasn't. I remember I fell off a ride, smashed my head open and ended up in hospital. I've still got a scar.'

That setback didn't stop him enjoying it nearly every year, although as an adult he now has a different outlook on his own personal Disney World. 'I used to think it took ages to get there but as I got older I realised it's a fucking shit hole. And it only takes half an hour to get down the M13.'

But for Danny growing up, it was one of the rare occasions where he stepped out from his East End village. Not that Danny has ever longed for an early exit from the area. 'I was born and bred in East London – in Canning Town, near West Ham. It's an absolute fucking shit hole but it's made me what I am today, giving me bollocks, and it's made me quite streetwise.'

His former schoolmate Julianna Sandy explained, 'When you come from the East End, you do tend to love your home area even after you've moved.'

Danny is immensely proud of where he is from. It's a place that has defined him, whether it's as a teenager getting into scrapes with his friends or as an adult living in the same area where he grew up as a kid. As an actor there has never been anyone who is so defined by his environment as Danny Dyer. He is the loveable, cocky East End hardman, and the rogue with the 'lock up your daughters, here comes Danny' swaggering charm.

This is his story.

Chapter Two

Dyer Straits

I'm not a fighter but, being brought up in East London, you've got to hold your hands up sometimes to get along

For anyone who's seen Danny's best-known films, including *Human Traffic*, *The Football Factory* and *The Business*, it shouldn't come as a shock to discover that he was a livewire growing up. What you see is what you get it seems. 'He was just the cocky kid that everyone liked,' revealed one of his schoolfriends, Wesley Crow, to the *Sun* years later.

Talking about the area and her school, his schoolmate Sandy recalled, 'Custom House was a nice enough area. The people were friendly. Our primary school [Scott Wilkie Primary] was good, but the secondary school that we went to was meant to be one of the worst in Newham. The teachers were mostly young and wanted the best for the children but a lot of kids lacked ambition.'

Danny's ambition at that time, it seemed, was to cause as much mischief as possible and play football. The sport, like for many young males in Britain, was to prove a welcome break from the daily educational grind. As soon as the classes ended and it was break time, Danny would rush from the classroom and head straight on to the nearby green.

He was usually picked as the goalkeeper, and the sight of a young Danny spouting colourful language at his defence was to be a regular occurrence. His history and PE teacher Tony Cole remembers him as a 'reasonable footballer' who played in the year team.

One of Cole's favourite memories involved taking the kids out of their East End comfort zone. 'I took them to Hampshire for the weekend. We visited Toby Balding's [famed British racehorse trainer] National Hunt stable in the morning and then went to Thruxton motor racing circuit in the afternoon. Most of the kids rarely left the East End.

'I can remember them getting excited because they saw some cows. Or "caass", as they would say,' Cole remembered fondly.

Attending Woodside Community School from 1988, which was one of the very few schools at the time not to have a uniform policy, saw young Danny quickly establish the loveable rogue and cheeky persona that would be for ever known to his scores of fans. Natalie Dorrington, who was two years below Danny, remembers him as 'a typical teenage lad at school ... not one of the quiet ones!'

He was certainly mischievous and something of a terror for the younger ones in his area. Sandy remembered, 'When I was younger he used to live near to me. He had a dog and whenever anyone went through the alley to get to school people would run! It was a kind of joke in our area: whenever you went that way you would look to see if the dog was there.'

While known for his hardman image, Danny insists that is not the real him. And it was one of his other lesser-known talents that made him fit in at school. 'You've just got to know how to stand up for yourself and not get taken for a mug [but] at school I was better at making people laugh. It's always the best way – get in with the bully, make him laugh and you've got everything sorted.'

Secondary school was to shape Danny's life for ever. It was there that he discovered that charm could help him side with all his classmates. 'Danny was an incredibly likeable kid at school' and 'got on with both the boffins and the baddies', according to classmate Joanne Batterbee.

'He is a genuine guy, what you see is what you get,' added another classmate, Lindsay Hamilton.

Cole remembers Danny as 'actually quite quiet but he was always on the verge. He kind of lit the blue touch paper and stood back. He was part of quite a lively tutor group with one or two "stars" in it. I taught him PE and history but had a lot to do with the class as I worked closely with them in my role as "behaviour support". He certainly wasn't a hardman. His assumed role still makes me laugh right now. But I'm absolutely thrilled he has made it big.'

Danny's charm also helped him when he was constantly pulled up for causing mischief in class or playing truant. His English and drama teacher, Jane Flynn, recalled,

'Danny was an amiable, mischievous lad at school. He could drive some staff crazy and turn on the charm with others. I liked him a lot and he was never anything other than pleasant, polite and always enthusiastic in my dealings with him.'

Danny was no angel, however. He was no stranger, as with most young boys in the area, to getting into physical scrapes. 'I've been battered a couple of times. It's part and parcel of growing up in East London. You need to fend for yourself from early on. I've had a few tear-ups, nothing major. I was knocked unconscious once, which was not very nice,' he said in an interview with the *Sun* in 2007.

What was becoming clearer and clearer with this restless and somewhat disillusioned young soul was that, whatever he did, trouble would never be far behind. And on one particular occasion it seemed to follow him from another world.

One weekend saw Danny and one of his pals deciding to daub graffiti over the trains with spray cans. Off the Jack-the-lads went at 1am to Stratford yard. They spent a couple of hours at the yard spray painting the trains ('Silly thing to do many moons ago when I was a young gun,' he has since remarked). When they finished they went down their normal escape route, which was jumping over a wall into a long alleyway.

At 3am, the alleyway suddenly became ominous; the shadows cloaked them in darkness while paranoid fear took over. Of course, the fact that Danny had begun indulging in marijuana was no doubt not helping matters.

But the pair sauntered on until they began to notice someone at the other end of the alleyway walking towards them. Looking back where they came from, they could see that it was a dead end with a big wall that was impossible to climb over. Yet the figure kept walking towards them.

Danny recounted the tale: 'We kept walking and he's getting closer. We looked down because we didn't really want to look. And as he's getting closer we can see that it's a monk. A monk! With all the fucking gear on and all that. So we walk past the monk, no word of a lie, ten seconds later he was fucking gone. There used to be an old monastery there, we later found out. There was definitely a ghost, no lying about that.'

It was, of course, a cause for concern for many that Danny could have ended up behind bars like many of the characters he would portray in his movies. However, he is adamant that, although he would probably be 'banged up' if things kept going the way they were, he always knew when to draw the line. 'I would never have got involved in guns. I was a bit of a tearaway when I was younger and I didn't know where my life was going so I got into crime, a bit of thieving and stuff. But shooting people in their own homes is a million miles away from what me and my friends were about. I've got a few friends who have done a bit of bird, but I know who the bad people are and I tend to stay away from them.'

His drama teacher agreed, saying, 'He was never a "Premier Division" rogue at the time and, fortunately, was not really involved with some of the "very hard" students. 'His mum held a close-knit family unit together despite the challenges of Danny's school misdemeanours at times.'

In an interview with lifestyle website AskMen.com, Danny insisted, 'I wasn't a bad kid. My dad left when I was young so I didn't have much discipline, not that I'm making excuses. I was always out and about and had a good time as a kid, so I've done all right.'

Despite his best assurances, it was not until fate stepped in that his parents could breathe a sigh of relief. At school, his drama teacher Flynn spotted a way out for Danny. Although acting was far from his mind growing up, it was clear to everyone who knew him that his show-off spirit and natural charisma were perfectly suited to acting.

While his first credited screen appearance was in 1993's *Prime Suspect 3*, there is video footage of a fresh-faced eleven-year-old Danny re-enacting a scene from popular 1980s children's football drama *Jossy's Giants* with his classmates. Filmed by a teacher in 1988 during a class trip, the footage shows a young Danny doing what he would later do in a score of films – getting into trouble because of his need to chat to girls.

The scene in question has a young Danny letting a goal in after being distracted by a group of girls. 'Danny was a real livewire but never mentioned acting. I dug the video out and couldn't believe he was on it. He looks so innocent,' recalled Crow to the *Sun*. 'He loved *Jossy's Giants* and acted out a scene but we had no idea he'd become famous.'

Like Crow, Batterbee was also surprised at Danny's future career. 'I was surprised that he made it as a successful actor as I don't remember him being particularly into drama at school,' she recalled.

His other schoolmate Sandy remembers it differently, however. 'When we were in secondary school Danny took part in some of the school plays and he was quite good. The teachers didn't think that he would be motivated enough though.'

However, his drama teacher Mrs Flynn saw that wasn't the case in the slightest. In fact, Danny was getting more and more of a taste of acting – until it became the sole reason for going to school. That and 'maybe seeing a fight after school', she once recalled, adding, 'He missed a lot of lessons at school but his attendance in drama was good. He was extremely energetic when he was interested in something but frustratingly indifferent when he wasn't and this obviously caused him problems with some subject areas and teachers.' For a teacher more used to hyperactive Danny than hardworking Danny, she knew that this could lead to something more than a hobby. 'Danny had a naturally serious and curious professional attitude towards his work in drama,' said Flynn. 'Although he had this natural talent and appeared very comfortable in all the roles he adopted, he was also a perfectionist in that he always wanted the performance to be better. For someone who was so headstrong and wilful in other areas of the school, he always took direction well, never argued and was keen to learn.'

However, Flynn was to notice something in Danny that

would rear its ugly head throughout his career – his little time for people who don't respect acting and don't put in the required effort. While Danny soaked up everything he could learn from his future co-stars like Dame Helen Mirren and Ray Winstone, he is less impressed with 'two-bob soap stars' and the like.

'His determination and personal desire for everything to be right sometimes caused him to become frustrated and a little intolerant of others but part of the learning process was to work constructively and supportively, despite problems and setbacks,' said Flynn. 'These are important attributes in any professional. I also have to say that, at that time, there was no "cockiness" about him with regard to his ability in drama – he just got on with it most of the time. He was refreshingly honest and uncontrived in his acting, and had a real sense of performance without any kind of precocity on stage.'

While he had finally found a passion and a creative outlet, the chance to pursue it as a career was one that he could never let enter his mind. He came from a working-class family in a working-class area. Actors, in Danny's mind, were people who had professional training, who had family ties to the industry and who had mates who wouldn't laugh if he told them that he wanted to be a thespian.

He told *AXM* magazine, 'It was the only thing I was ever good at in school – I was shit at everything else. The only reason I went to school was for drama. My teacher used to pull me aside at every lesson and tell me I was really talented and that I should really try to pursue it as a career. I thought, no fucking way – that wasn't going to happen. I had long, greasy curtains and for me, in East London, it wasn't the career path you'd take. You were either a boxer, a footballer or you'd end up painting and decorating, but I loved it so much.'

Flynn suggested an acting workshop every Sunday at the InterChange studios for disadvantaged young people. It was, in fact, a suggestion that she attempted after every drama lesson. Seeing no other 'avenues to go down in life', he took up her idea and started to go to the workshops.

'I was just concerned that he did as much drama as possible in his free time – it was something positive for him and, I guess, although it's the classic cliché, it was something which would hopefully "keep him off the streets" and out of trouble and temptation's way, as a wilful fifteen/sixteen-year-old in South Newham,' she said.

And so Danny went to the classes in Kentish Town, having to 'bunk the fare and jump the rails' at the tube station, as he never had any money.

It was a move that not only changed his life but also showed self-belief and self-reliance. 'It was such a solo thing. No one in my family has ever done it. It's not like I went down with my mates because my mates never did it. It's something I did on my own. I'm proud of that. No one has ever pushed me. No one has ever given me a leg up. I was never born with a fucking silver spoon in my mouth. Where I've got today is through my own graft and beliefs.'

And Flynn is modestly keen to play down her part, saying that it was all down to Danny. 'I wouldn't like to think that

I "pushed" Danny into acting, rather encouraged him to think of it as something he might want to have a go at, as he was clearly very talented, had a marketable "look" and image, and, most importantly, it seemed to be the only thing which he really enjoyed doing.'

Chapter Three

A Prime Talent

Cor, you're really good – Dame Helen Mirren
compliments Danny on his screen debut

It's not an overly simple observation to say that going to those workshops changed Danny's life. Through these classes he would not only quickly land himself an agent, but he would also find himself thrust into a world where he learned acting wasn't just about who was the biggest show-off. He learned about being free from everyday restraints and not caring what people think. He learned mime, improvisation and, more importantly, met people from all different walks and lives. 'I started to meet other people through other backgrounds, stuff like that, and I really enjoyed it.'

Talking about an alternative world where he had never taken up acting, he told Charlotte Church on his second appearance on her chat show, 'I'd probably be banged up, I reckon. But I found my talent at a young age. It got me away from that sort of world. I'm fucking useless at everything. I've got no back-up.'

What Danny had was a natural instinct for acting. He quickly realised it didn't matter how many years you spent at drama school, the key to acting was observing. 'I've learned everything from watching people,' he admits now.

And with years spent around some eccentric characters growing up, he had plenty to mine from. 'I come from the flats so I've got a few naughty people around me. Not necessarily my mates but, you know, people in the boozers and all that. So you just take little things. I never tell them that but it comes in handy,' he told the BBC.

When he got the part of soccer hooligan Tommy Johnson in 2004's *The Football Factory*, he didn't have to look far for inspiration. Thanks to his days out with his dad watching the West Ham games, he had enough real-life material to draw on. 'I've seen hooliganism on the terraces and it fascinated me. I'd rather have watched that than the match. It was nothing I ever got involved in, obviously. I'm just not that type of person. But I know people who are a part of that, so I didn't have to do any research for the role.'

Another thing he learned through the workshops and perfected through his career is harnessing real parts of himself for the role. Although he has repeatedly dismissed the hardman tag (while often playing up to it at times as well), he admits there are parts of him in every character he plays. He credits this for his getting parts over other actors at auditions – a gruelling process that every actor has to face in their lifetime and a practice that Danny, despite his fame, still has to go through on occasion.

'I'm not playing myself but the clever actor is bringing

out the best parts of himself and putting them into a role. That's what acting is about, whether you can change your accent or not, it's you,' he told the April 2007 issue of *Little White Lies*.

He explained the technique further to *The Student Pocket Guide* in 2008. 'I think that's what acting is – playing yourself. To win the part over everyone else, you bring something no one else can. All you can bring to the role is what's inside here,' he said, pounding his heart. 'You can go to drama school for three years and all come out the same robot and learn the same techniques – but, if I've got to laugh, I'll laugh the way I laugh, I'll cry the way I cry. Anyone can be an actor. It's about them being able to dig in there and get it. That's what the game is.'

It was a game he suddenly became a part of when he was spotted by an agent at InterChange studios. Impressed by his natural charisma, presence and burgeoning acting talent, he asked Danny to audition for a role in enduring British police show *Prime Suspect*.

When she heard about the *Prime Suspect* casting, a delighted Flynn saw it as Danny's perfect chance to break out. 'Danny had a marketable "look" as a young juvenile. When I learned that there was a casting taking place, I encouraged him to audition. The subject matter of the series was clearly going to be "earthy" and Danny could bring something very honest and real to it in his own way.

'Danny was not an academic and so was unlikely to follow the university route. A lot of very talented young people don't make it into the top six drama schools – it's very much a lottery – it was probably not a financially viable proposition for his family anyway – so this was an opportunity to be taken by someone like him. He had absolutely nothing to lose. I always advise students, even if very talented, against pursuing a career in acting, unless there is absolutely nothing else in the world which they could be happy doing.

'I believed this to be the case with Danny, he had the essential combination – an abundance of talent and a positive and quite professional attitude towards acting in the time that I had worked with him, and an employable "look" and background, and there was absolutely nothing else that he was likely to be happy doing at that stage. All he needed was that massively important ingredient – LUCK!'

But it was Danny's talent that landed him his first gig.

Veteran casting director Doreen Jones has casted some of the biggest British TV shows, including *Wallander*, *Prime Suspect* and *Brideshead Revisited*. She remembers clearly the day she met a very young, long-haired and hugely inexperienced Danny for 1993's *Prime Suspect 3*. She recalled, 'The brief was to look for a street kid who looked very young. He had to look rough but appealing. And I seem to remember I had a list of kids who I knew already – it was an all-right list but it wasn't a wonderful list. I remember his agent ringing me up, and she went on and on about this kid. So I said, "Send him in."'

For Danny this was the biggest test of his young life – he had a chance to show people that this was more than just a hobby. This was a way to carve out a career for himself, to leave behind his wilder life and appear on the TV in front of millions. Now all he had to do was convince Jones in a brief audition on the first time of asking.

'He looked great and very young for his age,' remembered Jones. 'Which is what we wanted, as he had to be around sixteen. Because of the context of the programme you obviously don't want a young kid.'

Jones was hugely impressed with the young Danny and decided he should meet the show's director David Drury.

'He was a nice lad. When I met him initially that first time he was very impressive. He was very determined and he had a passion. That was the most important thing.'

Although he had managed to get this far, it would all be for nothing if Drury felt that acting alongside such luminaries as David Thewlis and Dame Helen Mirren would be too much for an inexperienced actor. Luckily for Danny, Drury was very 'open to the idea of using a new actor who had never been on TV before', explained Jones. 'He was very good with new kids.'

Prime Suspect first began in 1991 and was produced by Granada Studios. It made Dame Helen Mirren a household name as no-nonsense DCI Jane Tennison – a character that has become 'like a friend' to her. Although a very complex friend, it seems.

'There are certain things about her that I do not like. I don't like her brutality; I don't like her extreme selfishness. Some things she does meet with my approval though. She walks on men and uses them – which is just what men often do to women. I think women are just as capable … I just reckon they do much more of it than they've so far confessed to.'

The two-part *Prime Suspect 3*, which was written by Lynda La Plante, focused on Tennison's move into the vice division. The first part was aired on British television on 19 December 1993, with the second part airing a day later.

Tennison is quick to land a very complex case involving the death of a young escort found burned to death at the home of drag queen Vera Reynolds (Peter Capaldi). The chief suspect is James Jackson (David Thewlis) – a pimp who grooms young homeless kids for a life of prostitution.

While it was a seedy storyline, Mirren was quick to point out that it wasn't far from reality after preparing for the episode by visiting the vice division at Charing Cross station. 'The really scary thing is that it isn't made up. Much of the content can be found in TV documentaries. We haven't needed to exaggerate for the sake of drama,' she said at the time.

Although Danny is only in a handful of scenes, he made a considerable impact not only on the show (his character is a vital one) but on his co-stars as well.

Danny recalls, 'I got a bit lucky and got a good break. I only had a couple of scenes in it but one of them was with Helen Mirren. It was a big moment for me when I sat opposite her and she started interrogating me but I felt at home with it. I wanted more of it. I started off and Helen said, "Cor, you're really good," which gave me a boost.'

'These kind of actors are very good with youngsters who haven't acted before. They're very helpful,' said Jones.

The performance that so impressed Mirren came from a scene that is one of the standout moments of *Prime Suspect 3*. Danny played a young rent boy called Martin

Fletcher. He has ties to the murdered escort and Tennison is determined to find out what Fletcher knows.

While Danny's character is older than his years in terms of the drama and abuse he has had to deal with, he's still just a young boy. Armed with petulant answers, he hardly takes the interrogation seriously, eyes darting mischievously across the room.

Tired of Fletcher's answers, Mirren delivers a knock-out speech. 'Now, you listen to me, Martin. You think you can play games with us, lie to us and it's all a joke. It's not. Colin Jenkins is dead. There's no one to claim his body, no one to even bury him. No one cares about Colin Jenkins but us – and you're next, Martin. You're the next little dead body we find down there, you know that?'

They turn out to be prophetic words as he is found dead days later from solvent abuse.

But if working with Helen was a joy, Danny found it a different experience working with another fantastically experienced actor.

The opening scene of *Prime Suspect 3* sees a young Danny running through the seedy streets of Soho chased by Thewlis's character. He is eventually caught and is then thrown to the ground. 'I don't know where he is,' he whimpers.

Like the interrogation scene, it is another intense moment in the film and a testament to Danny's talents that he was chosen to work with another one of Britain's finest actors.

Talking to *Blag*, he recalled, 'My first scene in acting was with David Thewlis, who I think is fucking brilliant.

He plays my pimp, and the first real scene is him chasing me down the street and him grabbing hold of me, whacking me up against the fence and kissing my mouth. They threw me in at the deep end – it's quite an intense scene and I was shitting myself.'

What didn't make it easier was how David prepared for the role. While both stayed at the same London hotel the night before, they were hardly bosom buddies. In a bid to add some tension to the scene and to get Danny's creative juices flowing, Thewlis decided to teach the young actor a trick or two about getting into your role.

As they were coming down together in the lift that morning, Thewlis refused to acknowledge the young Danny. He even purposely ignored him all the way to the set. Being new to the game, and not someone who is used to being ignored, Danny was understandably irked by it all. 'Thewlis is quite method so he didn't talk to me. I was thinking, You prick. It's only later when you realise what he was doing. He was shitting me up a little bit before the scene. And I appreciate that.'

It was an accomplished screen debut that shocked not only his experienced co-stars but also his friends and family – because it was clear Danny had a natural talent. It can't be an easy task standing out in an episode that featured not only Mirren and Thewlis, but also the likes of Capaldi, Ciaran Hinds, Mark Strong and Jonny Lee Miller.

Like Danny's drama teacher, Jones also refuses to take any credit for Danny's success. 'I don't believe in all that rubbish about discovering people. It's our luck that they happened to cross our paths and give us the chance to push them on their way a bit. It's them that's got the talent, not us.'

For Danny, though, it meant he had finally found his life calling. 'I always felt at home on set even though I knew nothing about it technically. I knew it was where I was meant to be.'

Chapter Four

An Actor's Life for Me

I like to show off

Danny told Russell Brand on his chat show in 2006, 'I got picked out from there by an agent who wanted me to audition for *Prime Suspect*. It was my first audition and I got the part. I played a rent boy, got paid fifteen hundred quid for a week's work, worked with Helen Mirren and thought, This is a piece of fucking piss. This is great, so that's how it started.'

And he had every reason to be confident at the time. He had gone toe-to-toe with the best and had passed with flying colours. But if he was to think this acting lark was easy, he was to get a shock to the system. But that's for later because, for now, he was on top of the world.

While Danny comes across like your cheeky mate down the pub who has been hit by the lucky stick, he is actually someone who is intently obsessed with proving himself as an actor. Intensely confident in his abilities, he told this author in 2005 about how he doesn't like being stuck in the same acting gang that frequent Guy Ritchie films. 'I can do that stuff in my sleep. I can bloody well act, I know I can. I still feel I need to prove it to people though.'

But Danny wasn't just counting on his natural talent to sustain acting as a career. He was a keen enthusiast on studying every actor he appeared alongside – good or bad. He was, and still is, determined to show everyone that the little boy from the streets of Custom House can make it as a talented actor.

However, there was a potential stumbling block and his former drama teacher Flynn spotted it straight away. She explained, 'The significant thing which he couldn't do was speak any kind of approximation of standard English at that time. I did point out that it might be sensible for him to get some regular and intensive quality professional voice training in order that he could become more versatile and have more to offer. I realised that there were financial implications in this and was not sure that it was a possibility at the time, so just encouraged him to think about it as something to invest in for the future, so that he could avoid becoming typecast.'

While he couldn't afford to attend any kind of accent or dialogue lessons, what Danny did do instead was watch everyone like a hawk – mentally taking notes on what worked and what didn't. 'Now and then you come across an actor and, fucking hell, he's brilliant, and you just sit there and study them. Watch everything they do and the way they approach it. You watch how they snap out of character when the director says cut.

'There's an actor called Mark Rylance – he's a

Shakespearean actor who I did a thing called *Loving* with [a 1995 BBC2 TV movie]. I was like the country boy and he was the butler. He was just fucking brilliant. He had this dictaphone that he used to walk around with. He used to listen to it and snap in and out of character like that. I just found him fascinating. Another one was Helen Mirren. Just little things that you pick up on.'

Not that he was full of admiration for all his co-stars. Speaking in 2007, he said, 'The majority of actors who I've worked with I think are shit. I'd never tell them that but I just think, What's the fuss about? I don't get it, you know.'

What *Prime Suspect* taught him, and indeed the countless shows that he would appear in following his applauded screen debut, was the ability to do less on screen. Actors on stage and screen find both mediums incredibly different. The former encourages you to be larger than life, to project your body and voice for all to see and hear – while the latter expects the complete opposite. Film is about subtlety and the manipulation of the camera.

For such a natural show-off, it's surprising that Danny prefers the studied nuances of film rather than the stage – but some of his more acclaimed performances are ones when he is doing little. His role as Martin Fletcher in *Prime Suspect 3* or as Frankie in 2005's *The Business* relied heavily on using his eyes to convey a scene.

'What I learned is to do fuck all. It's all about being still. That's a lot more powerful than fucking throwing yourself around. It can be a more powerful crying scene when you just have one tear rolling down your eye than just sobbing your heart out, snot everywhere. It's just more subtle.'

Indeed, *Variety* magazine praised Danny's low-key performance in *The Business*, saying, 'Dyer, who first came to attention as Moff in *Human Traffic*, makes Frankie a much more shaded character than his confident voiceover suggests, and carries the viewer along in a subtly slow-burning performance.'

'Lots of tricks to acting. I think it's a real art just using your eyes,' Danny continued. 'That's the key to acting for me. That's why I prefer films. Lots of things like how to use the camera and how you're meant to forget the camera is there but actually it's the one thing you've got to play up to. It's the one thing that captures every emotion and I quite like that.'

Luckily for Danny, there would be plenty of experiences in front of the camera after the success of *Prime Suspect 3*. Although he would say in interviews that he was fourteen when he got his big break in the detective drama series, he was actually fifteen, and sixteen when his appearance was aired. As a sixteen-year-old, he had his foot in the door and, buoyed by his debut, it wasn't long before he was given a second opportunity to impress.

His next role was in another British detective show. Based on the novels by Edith Pargeter (under the alias Ellis Peters), *Cadfael* revolved around a Welsh Benedictine monk at Shrewsbury Abbey during the twelfth century. Despite wanting to live the quiet life tending to his herbs, Cadfael is constantly forced to use his master sleuthing skills.

In the 1994 episode 'Leper of St Giles', the detective monk has to come to the aid of a young knight called Joscelyn, who is the prime suspect for the murder of Baron Huon de Domville. The baron was due to marry the young heiress Iveta de Massard – somewhat reluctantly in her case, as she and Joscelyn were embroiled in their own passionate love affair.

While his role lacked the impact of his screen debut, it still gave Danny the chance to star alongside Sir Derek Jacobi (Cadfael) and Sean Pertwee. Danny played a recovering leper thanks to the detective monk's healing herbs. He appears briefly in two scenes and, like *Prime Suspect*, he is almost unrecognisable from the cheeky pin-up that has snared him a sizeable female fan base.

Again, it was Doreen Jones who cast him in the show. 'That was only a small part,' she said. 'I think it was before *Prime Suspect* came out and I didn't really think about it too much. I was like, "Oh, Danny can do that."'

He appears on screen right from the start, with his fresh-faced features, skinny legs and floppy haircut. Danny's one speaking line is delivered competently enough. He tells the mysterious leper of the episode's title that 'God has punished him for whipping you'.

Cadfael was shot in Hungary and, because of his age, Danny had to be chaperoned by his dad. During a commentary for *Outlaw*, he told director Nick Love, 'I was a leper. Couple of lines. Young guy then but it was one of my first real cracks of the whip.'

He would work again in Hungary once more in the 2006 horror comedy *Severance*, and both times were a less than pleasant experience. 'I'd worked in Hungary before on *Cadfael*,' he told *Film Review* in 2006. 'I didn't like it then either.'

On the *Severance* 'Making Of', he went on to explain further. 'Hungary didn't really do it for me, I'll be straight with ya, you know what I mean. I'm a proper British, English cockney lad. I like the rain, like me roast dinner. I just like sitting in my house watching my telly.'

For Danny, who is traditionally typecast as a cockney rogue, *Cadfael* was one of the few roles where he has managed to escape East London – and a period piece to boot. That is something Danny regrets he has not done enough. 'I want to play a king. I'd love to play an aristocrat, a posh boy or something to really freak people out. But I just don't get things like that. I'm just a peasant out of East London.'

The next two years were busy ones for Danny – on paper at least. He may have only been scoring small roles but his face was constantly being seen on some of British TV's biggest shows and he continued to star alongside some of the country's biggest names. He starred in a 1995 episode of *A Touch of Frost* entitled 'Dead Male One', where he found himself once again in a police interrogation room being grilled by British acting royalty – this time Sir David Jason. Shorn of his long hair that he had sported in *Prime Suspect* and *Cadfael*, and looking more like the Danny Dyer that his fans know today (albeit far more baby faced), his character Shaun is a young football-obsessed fan who attacks someone he wrongly blames for putting his club's star player in a coma.

But, while he was once again in a police interrogation room, the character of Shaun was miles away from his *Prime Suspect* character. His is a charming, naive and affable performance.

While his subsequent TV roles were playing characters very much in the laddish mould, there would be something different in each performance – whether it be the touching and powerful performance as half of a Burberry Bonnie and Clyde in an episode of *Thief Takers* or as a protective brother in an episode of cult TV series *Highlander*. While his performance may have been wasted in the first episode of the show's sixth and final season – which fans consider the series' worst season – it still remains a curio item nonetheless. As do many of his earlier appearances, including recurring roles in *Children's Ward* and *Soldier Soldier* – as well as the famous Coca Cola advert, which saw Danny denounce a rival soft drink with the damning verdict: 'It tastes like chicken.'

They are like watching personal home video tapes of someone growing before your eyes – adapting to each new role with ease but at the same time trying to define who they actually are. That was something he didn't know, but he was enjoying himself trying a variety of disguises without constrictions, long before the success of *The Football Factory* launched Danny into a lucrative, albeit hard to wrestle out of, niche.

While he may have grown up to resent the medium of TV, for now he was having the time of his life. He was getting paid well and it was a tiring but incredibly rewarding apprenticeship, although in a 2008 interview he did reveal that there was one show he never got to star in – the long-running BBC medical drama *Casualty*. 'I remember I used to be up for it all the time and I never got a part in the cunt.'

But Danny was to experience another important lesson in acting. Though the jobs were coming in thick and fast, the life of an actor is rarely a steady one. Periods of huge amounts of work can be followed up with a barren spell that can test even the most unshakeable of confidences.

Danny was to face such a test at a time when he was just learning his trade. It was to be a steep learning curve. He told journalist Tony Gill in 2004, 'I went through a period of getting loads of work when I was a child actor, as I had a real baby face. Then I starting growing up a little bit, my voice broke, I shot up, but I couldn't shave yet, so I wasn't an adult actor or a child actor, I was caught in the middle. So I had a real shitty period of nothing, and I had a kid really young as well, so I had to be earning money. I went through this stage of thinking, I'm in the wrong game, I need to go back to labouring and all that.'

It was a crushing blow to his esteem and it looked like Danny was to be yet another child actor tossed on the scrapheap when they outgrew their roles.

Chapter Five
Stopping Traffic

Nice One, Bruvvvaaaa

Dani Charlotte Dyer was born in 1996, much to delight of her beaming parents, Danny Dyer and Joanne Mas. Their relationship was, and to an extent still is, a complicated and fiery one, and one that will be looked at further in a later chapter.

For the first time since his acting debut, Danny's personal life was taking precedence over his career. While the jobs came in quick and fast after *Prime Suspect*, they had since dried up. To make ends meet, the nineteen-year-old had begun working on a construction yard. It was something of a comedown for Danny, who thought acting would have saved him from a life that he had seen all too much growing up. He was no longer the talk of his class or the town – the kid who managed to break out through acting.

'I've done these shitty jobs. I've done labouring and stuff like that. My old man's been doing it for twenty years. He stuck it out because he had no choice.'

Making the ends meet was admirable though, because Danny was not doing it for himself but for his new family. Danny was now a dad and he knew that just doing nothing in the hope that a great part would fall on his lap was no longer an option. So he had to do what work he could get. 'Loading skips. I'd started acting but had to do other jobs on the side. I hated it. When people were grafting on places and ripping all the shit out I had to put in the skip. That was it. I was the lowest ebb on the ladder. Horrible.'

One thing being a parent did to Danny, however, was to help curb his hard-partying lifestyle. Before he was able to get into clubs, Danny became an ever-present figure on the streets around Custom House, taking drugs and making a nuisance of himself. 'Everyone in my area was doing it. Everyone. You've got to do it,' he explained. 'It's hard not to do it and you miss out on a lot if you don't.' Not that taking drugs, E in particular, was something he was blasé about. 'You've got to have something going on in your head to take it in the first place. It's a big risk taking an E.'

But in an article with *This Is London* in 1999 he admitted that being a dad saved him 'free-styling from the edge'. 'I'm glad I've done it now. I've got it out of my system. My mind was going to mush. But it's such a good buzz that you can click back into it straight away. Even now when I listen to a good tune, I get that little rush up my spine. But I couldn't do the E thing any more,' he added in a 1999 interview with *Time Out*.

Not that he had stopped completely. Drugs were still to

play a large part in Danny's life and his career in general – because that breakout part that every actor longs for was coming when he least expected it. And while he would utilise all the skills he learned, his own instinct that you bring yourself to each role was the one he would fully lean on for one of his most iconic screen roles. The film was *Human Traffic*, and the part was the irrepressible Moff. It was to transport Danny back into the limelight and he would never again be one of those actors that he feared the most – the ones that you would spot and grapple with the name on the tip of your tongue and say, 'Wait, I know who that is. Isn't that … Oh, how do I know him?'

The tracksuited, East London-born Moff was a career-defining part for Danny and the canny twenty-one-year-old knew it. 'I totally identified with Moff, he's a great character. I was a nutter like him when I was younger.'

Written and directed by newcomer Justin Kerrigan, the kinetic and frantic movie about the exploits of five teenagers over a rave-fuelled weekend in Cardiff was a milestone for teenage ravers over the world, who finally had a movie that didn't talk down to them or revile their pastime. This was a film for clubbers made by clubbers – the *Trainspotting* for the pill-popping generation, with a soundtrack featuring dance stars Fatboy Slim, Orbital and Brainbug. It even gained the backing of one of the era's biggest super-DJs. 'I think it's going to be a cult film,' proclaimed Pete Tong.

The five central protagonists were Jip, Koop, Lulu,

Nina and Moff – characters who worked eight hours a day, five days a week in jobs they despised. The weekend represented their escape from the boredom of their jobs and freedom from the restrictions of the daily grind.

After John Simm (Jip) joked with journalists that they were always taking E during filming, some of the actors were quick to shy away from talking about their real-life drug experiences. Simm remembered saying to a journalist, 'All right, I'll tell you what happened. I'll tell you how we did it. Every morning we'd come on set and we'd have two Es every single day. All the extras had to have an E before they came in, and some were only thirteen! And she was like, "Really?"'

Danny played Moff, the son of a policeman and a part-time drug dealer. He was a standout character and one for which Danny needed to draw on all his life experience. 'I think people will want to see it because it's a representation of their lives. No one wants to say they've had anything to do with Es. But this film had brought it to life, it tells you what your son and daughter are doing every weekend, whether you like it or not.'

He had a partner in crime in his co-star Shaun Parkes. The then twenty-six-year-old actor was scared to show his church-going mother. 'What am I meant to say to her?' he said in an interview with the *Evening Standard*. 'Someone is going to have to go up to her in church and tell her what I've been saying and I'm going to have shit to deal with.'

Lead actor John Simm, who was best known at the time

for his role in Jimmy McGovern's *The Lakes* and now for time-travelling show *Life On Mars*, agreed. He knew they were making a culturally relevant film – one that would deal realistically regarding the E generation. Simm remembered, 'It's the biggest culture of our times. It's the biggest thing that's ever happened to our generation. If you go out and take E and listen to the music, you're going to have the best night of your life, and if you don't experience it you're going to be sorry.'

Despite it earning a cult following, the film was a hard sell to begin with. Producer Allan Niblo said at the time, 'We don't have the same infrastructure as the American indie scene, which is thriving. We had actors, we had American interest and yet nobody would back it.

'People rejected the script because it was too original. The first thing everyone said was, "What's the structure? We don't understand this." People wanted a different film. "You can have it but take out all the drug bits and just have a love story."'

Director Justin Kerrigan adds, 'We tried everybody and went everywhere looking for money. You name it – Channel 4, Arts Council, BFI, even the bloody Lottery – nobody would give us a penny. Why? Because there was no moral lesson in the film, nobody dies or gets screwed up – which they interpreted as us condoning drug use – and because of what they called "gratuitous bad language". And then there was me, an unknown quantity.'

Kerrigan, who first snuck into raves when he was

fourteen, was determined to make a film that reflected accurately the rave culture. Indeed, the 1995 BBC drama *Loved Up*, which was part of the *Love Bites* season, was not well received by the clubbing community.

Directed by Peter Cattaneo, who would helm *The Full Monty* two years later, the TV movie focuses on a young woman called Sarah (played by Lena Headey, who would go on to star in her own action show *Terminator: The Sarah Connor Chronicles*) and her new relationship with a serial clubber named Tom (Ian Hart). The rave community sniped that the film seemed to blame Sarah's failure to commit to Tom on the clubbing culture, rather than the result of her dysfunctional upbringing. Critics seemed to disagree, with *Variety* praising the film's realistic tone, saying, 'Despite the vast quantities of pills popped, the pic never gets sidetracked into preaching about drugs.'

That film also featured Danny. So, before he was in danger of being typecast as an East End hardman, he was clearly seen as the ideal choice for a drug dealer!

Kerrigan said, '*Human Traffic* is my way of trying to give this generation a voice. I've been part of that culture from the early days, and I met one of my best friends and had some of the best times of my life through going clubbing.'

They did eventually manage to get financial backing – £5,000 from the Welsh Film Council and £25,000 of film stock and processing, which came from winning the DM Davies Award – which he had done with his graduation film. As a budget it was a meagre one at best – but Niblo and co. did manage to secure further funding from overseas in America, and from Irish Screen, which was headed up by former head of drama at the BBC, Michael Wearing.

It wasn't just the financial backing that Kerrigan struggled with. One of his cast members, Lorraine Pilkington, was warned off at first by her agent. But finally the then twenty-four-year-old director did manage to assemble his cast, a blend of unknowns and rising stars – all of whom were working for a fraction of their normal fees.

According to Danny, the audition process was different to the one he was normally used to. In a revealing interview with *Attitude*, he said, 'The first question I was asked in the audition was, "Do you take drugs?" And I was like, "Yes, I love drugs." Most people denied having taken them at the interview. The director saw a lot of people, big actors at the time, and they denied taking drugs, which made him go, "Thanks, see you later." He wanted someone who knew what they were talking about. It was six weeks of debauchery. It's weird for me to watch it now.'

Attempting to tackle a mainstream youth culture that has largely been ignored by the film industry, Kerrigan's film is an admirable and hugely entertaining one. The highs and lows are both reflected in the film. Danny's character in particular is cannily ambivalent. Is Moff stumbling into the speakers, mumbling, 'Who are you people?', completely wasted and paranoid, a hint that the party is over, or is it a regular ending of a weekend that is set on repeat for a long time to come?

'Paranoia is such a personal thing. I think what Justin's realised is that everyone does go through that. We've all got paranoias in the film, and not necessarily because of drugs. It heightens your real paranoia,' said Parkes, while promoting the movie.

Not for the first time would a Danny Dyer film attract controversy from 'Middle England' media about the depiction of the other side of Britain. Not that Danny cared, however. 'A lot of people ain't going to like it. If they want to do live debate programmes on it, I'm prepared to go on.' But a live TV drug debate featuring Danny sadly didn't happen! 'This film shows the way it is every weekend. If people don't like it, bollocks to them,' he added.

It was a hectic shoot. The house party scene, in particular, saw the extras struggle to come to terms with where the script ended and real life began. Extras ended up getting drunk, with some getting together romantically. Well, sort of romantically.

'They were shagging in the loo, on the snooker table. Meanwhile, we had to drink Red Bull and concentrate on the next take,' remembers Parkes.

Danny was indulging in more than Red Bull, however. He told the *Daily Star* in a 2006 interview, 'I realised that the key to playing my character was to have experienced what it is like to be high on coke and Es. You cannot recreate the effects of ecstasy. So that was the key and we decided to celebrate it. I ripped the arse out of that character for six weeks. I was taking Es on the set every day. I loved the honesty of that in *Human Traffic*. It was real, that's why I loved it.'

It was a chaotic set and a stressful one to boot. Because it was an extremely low-budget shoot with an inexperienced director and a cold Cardiff setting, the conditions weren't perfect for the actors. However, Kerrigan's enthusiasm helped propel them along.

Lorraine Pilkington told *Time Out* shortly before the film came out, 'Justin is completely driven. Working on the film was like dealing with his soul. There were breaking points for all of us during filming – there was no money, it was late at night, we were freezing, we were starving and the actor in you goes, "I'm not doing this any more. I'm not doing it." And then Justin would just look at you and you'd think, How can I not do it for him? Once we started, it was almost like we'd agreed to do *anything*.' However, even Pilkington concedes that she 'would never have worked those hours in those conditions for any other script or any other director'.

Kerrigan's enthusiasm papered over the cracks but the budget was a sticking issue for the cast, who had to endure less than professional conditions. Even the extras, many of whom were Justin's friends, were paid not in cash but in drink and cigarettes.

Parkes recalls, 'Justin was great but, if it had been a first job for any of us, I think we would have given up acting.'

It was pure DIY filmmaking, with Simm revealing, 'All the money went on screen. A lot of people working on it were just Justin's friends, they'd never worked on a film before.'

The film's budget even hit a memorable scene featuring Moff masturbating to a porn magazine. 'In the script I'm having a wank and the two women come to life so it's like this sort of fantasy. I've got to fucking wank but I have two birds all over me and all that. But when we get to the day, and because there's no money, the birds they get in were two old brasses from Cardiff. And then you've got to do the scene in front of forty people with clipboards. You've just to get on with it. But it's like a nightmare.'

And, if Danny thought that scene would end when the day was finished, he was very much mistaken. There was the small matter of the *Human Traffic* premiere in the summer of 1999. It was a moment that he had longed for years, attending the premiere of his own film with the closest members of his family. All those years of paying his dues in the acting world – the small roles, the countless rejections and the low pay – was now worth it. He was a bona fide movie star and now everyone could see it. But nothing comes easy for Danny and for his first big-screen appearance he had to sit with, among others, his mother and Nana as they watched him pleasuring himself in the film. 'I just sat there squirming, thinking, Oh, God,' he recalled.

Another gripe for Danny while filming was that Cardiff's nightlife couldn't compare to London's. 'It was just a complete shambles. People are well up for it but there's twenty-year-olds walking about with 'taches, know what I mean?'

Recalling his experiences filming in Cardiff to Welsh

celebrity Charlotte Church, he said, 'I can't really remember [Cardiff] when I did that film. It was just chaos, absolute debauchery. It was six weeks of absolute mayhem but we made a little film in between.' He added, 'That's a nutty film. I loved making that film, man. It was a great moment. It was my first film and there was lots of improvising. I had an opportunity to show what I can do. Basically, it was me off my fucking nut. So I sort of got famous for being an absolute raving lunatic. Mad times.'

What got them through was their reliance on each other. The cast were extremely close and none displayed any airs and graces – unsurprising really because this was hardly a film set for divas. Talking about the on-screen closeness with the cast, Simm revealed, 'It's no great acting feat for me. It's like that, it really is.'

However, things didn't look rosy for the film when shooting finished. The film's first cut ran at a staggering and bum-numbing three hours, and producer Niblo was understandably worried. 'We knew we had to lose an hour. We took fifty-six weeks to edit it. We'd only booked sixteen. We couldn't afford that! [We were] convinced we had a turkey on our hands. Everyone was getting paranoid and depressed.'

Despite the setbacks, the film was a box-office hit in the UK, taking £2.2 million. Because of that success, the US distribution rights were snapped up by indie film giants Miramax. Like *Trainspotting*, it announced a new host of rising British stars and a director who was hailed by Miramax's Harvey Weinstein as 'one of the most exciting filmmakers of his generation'.

In 2002, a new version of the film was released on DVD with a 'modernised' soundtrack, under the title *Human Traffic – Remixed*, though the launch was marred by internal wrangling over the edition. The *Remixed* edition featured new scenes from the cutting-room floor but at the expense of several scenes from the original film. The 1994 anti-Criminal Justice and Public Order Act demonstration and the riots that were the subsequent result were removed from the original title sequence. Their original inclusion by Kerrigan was to make an implicit political statement.

A furious Kerrigan explained, 'I joke about it. How I signed over the copyright for a pound and then never even saw the pound. When I finished I was £25,000 in debt. I've never made a penny from the film. Legally, I don't have a leg to stand on, but I signed a contract because I was very naive and very broke. Now I'm just broke.'

While relationships between directors and producers are normally fraught ones at best, Kerrigan and Niblo had a shared past. Kerrigan struck up a mentor–pupil relationship with his partner back at Newport film school. The producer was the person who pushed Justin into writing about his experiences in the rave culture. Because of the film's huge cult following, it was unsurprising that Niblo wanted a sequel, but the original had fared 'spectacularly badly overseas'. That failure could be attributed to nearly fifteen minutes of cuts and redubbed scenes to appeal to an American audience, including Nina's line that was she looking forward to getting into some hardcore Jerry Springer, rather than the original line, 'Richard and Judy'.

In a 1999 feature in the *Guardian*, it is stated that the budget was officially £2.2 million. However, Kerrigan was quick to call it a retrospective sum. 'Nobody ever told me I had that much to make it, that's for sure ... I personally raised the money for *Human Traffic* when everyone else turned it down.'

There was even talk of a *Human Traffic*, the TV series, but luckily for Danny it never transpired. 'It's an hour-and-a-half movie so you don't want to milk it. There's only so much talking bollocks you can do,' he explained.

The film was warmly received by critics, with many glossing over some of the more simplistic narrative aspects in favour of praising the energetic debut of Kerrigan and his cast. And it was Dyer who was singled out for his performance by many review sites, with the BBC calling him 'fun to watch'.

In fact, Danny, with his many films under his belt, is still known for his role as Moff. He told the *Guardian*, 'The one I hear the most is from *Human Traffic*. People come up to me and yell, "Nice one, bruvvaaa!" And women come up to me and say, "I can't wait to see your fanny" [referring to a catchphrase from *The Football Factory*].'

Danny's abiding memory of the movie is one that served as a snapshot of not just the moment his film career took off, but also of a time of youthful innocence. This was more than just a film for the cast; it was a chance to relive a youth they were leaving behind.

'That's why I'm glad I made this film – it reminds me of all the times I've had, the fucking great times,' says Danny. 'I've got it on film, it's there. It's a great buzz to see it.'

Chapter Six

Give Danny a Supporting Hand

There's a lot of fucking rejection in acting

The role of Moff put Danny Dyer firmly in the spotlight because it showed what he was capable of. He was now seen as one of the country's brightest talents and certainly one of the more colourful characters. Careerwise, things couldn't get any better.

While he wanted to latch on to his newfound fame with both hands, he was keen not to jump into another Moff-type role. He realised how important it was to show that he could do things other than play a pill head. In fact, while it took him longer than he thought it would to play a lead in a big movie (*The Football Factory* was to come five years later), this was arguably his finest time in terms of stretching his acting ability. For a little while, at least.

First up was the harrowing WWI drama *The Trench*. It told the story of a group of soldiers stuck in a trench forty-eight hours before the Battle of the Somme in

1916 – one of the largest battles in the war and one that saw 1.5 million casualties.

Directed by William Boyd, it starred Danny, *EastEnders* pin-up Paul Nicholls and a pre-James Bond Daniel Craig. Danny puts in a strong performance, as do the majority of the cast. But the critics were left unimpressed with Boyd's direction, condemning the stage-bound set as too obvious. That said, the final scene where the young soldiers go over the top is an incredibly moving one.

Up next was 2000's *The Borstal Boy*, and for Danny it showed a different side to his talents. Based on the memoirs by acclaimed Irish poet and political activist Brendan Behan, the film focuses on the sixteen-year-old Republican's experiences after he is caught on his way to Liverpool on a bombing mission in 1942. He is sent to Borstal, a reform institute for young offenders in East Anglia.

Directed by Peter Sheridan, brother of *My Left Foot* writer/director Jim Sheridan, the drama centres on Behan (played by American actor Shawn Hatosy) as he struggles to adapt to living with people he considers his sworn enemies, as well as coming to terms with his sexuality.

In a role that is miles away from Moff and Danny's subsequent starring roles, Dyer plays Charlie Millwall, an incarcerated, openly homosexual sailor, who fights for Behan's affections with the warden's daughter (Eva Birthistle) – a love triangle that seemed to have been invented for the movie.

'It's a gay love story,' said Danny. 'But it's not a gay film. It's got a bit of everything.'

The script shocked Danny because he had different ideas when he heard the film's title. 'I got a message from Jim Sheridan. He rung me up and said he was doing a film called *Borstal Boy* and he wanted me to do it and all this. I got really excited about being a Borstal boy, running around beating everyone up, until I got the script and I was a gay sailor. I thought, Whoa, I'm going to have to act now.'

In the film's 'making of', Danny said of his character, 'He's a young boy, seventeen, who knows where he is sexually. He's gay and that's it. To be openly gay in Borstal must be a nightmare but that has made him a strong character.'

Although Danny admits that a 'whole day dressed up as a woman' was hard to take, it was nothing compared to the scene where he has a lingering kiss with Hatosy. Speaking before shooting it, he said, 'I think the most challenging scene is going to be when I kiss Brendan. A full-on passionate kiss is going to be heavy. When I do it, I know I'm going to do it well because there is no other way. Once I've done that I can do anything. There is nothing else in this game that could frighten me. Just got to put my tongue in his mouth!'

While critics were almost universal in their praise for Danny's performance, the film itself received a lukewarm critical reaction. The chief concern was how 'loose' the adaptation was. The *New York Magazine* in particular felt that Sheridan was too flowery with Behan's life and failed to signpost the 'legendarily raucous, Guinness-chugging writer he would become'. The review also had a problem with the ending, where Behan 'ambles into the mist like someone who has a rosy future all mapped out for him'. Indeed the film's rose-tinted ending makes it hard to believe that in real life Behan would return to jail on more than one occasion.

What was obvious, though, was that, like his performance in *Human Traffic*, no matter the billing status, Danny was someone who stood out regardless of how many lines he had. Arguably, Danny is at his best when, to use a footballing analogy, he's brought off the bench as an impact sub. Hatosy has appeared in films such as *The Faculty*, *John Q* and *Alpha Dog*, and in TV shows such as *Six Feet Under*, *ER* and *My Name Is Earl* – yet he was completely overshadowed by Danny's performance.

The *Boston Globe*, in particular, raved about Danny's performance. 'Danny Dyer consistently eclipses Hatosy, rising far above the script to deliver a layered performance that smoulders. His openly gay Charlie is by far the most interesting point in a manufactured cinematic love triangle.'

Danny then showed his lighter side in the charming British comedy *Greenfingers*, which saw him reunited with an old friend – Dame Helen Mirren. His *Prime Suspect* co-star was delighted to see Danny when she came on the set.

'I love her to bits,' said Danny. 'She came in and said, "There he is, my boy," and gave me a big cuddle. She's perfect to me, a great actress, great person, good heart, kind, gentle and graceful. When she accepted her Oscar [for her performance as the Queen in 2007], she couldn't have delivered a better speech. She must have been nervous but she came across as very elegant and very in control.'

An elegant statement by Dyer and one that proves how fond he is of Mirren – a testament to how she treats her young co-stars. Of course, as you would expect from Danny, he almost undid his good work in other interviews. 'I'd bang Helen Mirren,' he has said in the past. Not as elegant, you would probably agree.

Alongside his reunion with Mirren, his latest role gave him a chance to act alongside future Hollywood star Clive Owen. Danny plays Tony, one of three convicts who are transported to a low-security prison. Owen's Colin Briggs and Adam Fogerty's Raw are the other convicts. The charming British comedy had Danny in fine, roguish form. Within minutes of his first appearance, he has his eyes on the prison's tea lady (played by Lucy Punch).

Directed by Joel Hershman, the film is loosely based on a true story about the prisoners of the Cotswolds minimum-security prison HMP Leyhill. A big believer in redeeming convicts to make sure they are not repeat offenders, Prison Governor Hodge (played by Warren Clarke) wants to teach them skills for the real world. Despite his reluctance, Briggs discovers a love for gardening thanks to his inmate Fergus Wilks (David Kelly). Seeing a chance to make headlines, the four are recruited by the warden to make a showpiece garden for the prison. Duped into thinking she is checking on a fan's garden, garden expert and celebrated author Georgina

Woodhouse (Mirren) is shocked to be escorted to the prison. However, she is soon marvelling at the garden that the inmates have planted. Developing a soft spot for them, she endorses the garden and gets them to help tend to her rich clients' gardens. Soon, the novice gardeners are granted the chance to compete in England's highest flower-show award, the Hampton Court Flower Show – which is attended by Her Majesty. Complications arise, however, when one of her rich clients' mansions is burgled and all fingers point at Danny's character. Although discovering at the end that he was innocent, the audience are supposed to think that he is guilty so feel no remorse when Danny escapes from the prison and is never seen again. Despite being thrown out of the show, the inmates compete again the following year and their garden receives a royal blessing.

While never a success at the box office, it has a lazy Sunday-afternoon-TV feel about it, which should suggest a constant fixture on the TV schedule. Even the prison wardens – so often the bad guy of British movies – are nice and cuddly.

Each film after *Human Traffic* exhibited a depth in Danny's canon – whether as a soldier, a gay convict or a charming rogue. Danny was growing as an actor. They may not have been huge parts but they were ones that proved there was more to him than portraying a pill-popping raver. That was until his next project.

In 2001, he made a TV movie called *Is Harry on the Boat?* – a raucous lager-fuelled comedy about a group of 18–30 workers in Ibiza. Because of the huge success of Sky

One's reality show *Ibiza Uncovered*, Sky were keen to make a fictional version of the show. The *Media Guardian* announced details of the film, saying it 'follows a group of twenty-something tour reps sleeping their way around Ibiza during a summer of drug taking and clubbing, before a tragedy forces them to sober up'.

It was based on the book by Colin Butts – with the odd title a cockney rhyming slang sexual reference for ejaculation on the face.

Danny starred alongside Ralf Little, Will Mellor, Daniela Denby-Ashe and his future fiancée Davinia Taylor. As you can imagine, Danny was going to take to the sun, sex, sea and sangria lifestyle of Ibiza pretty easily.

Mellor recalled, 'I thought he was a great actor. We got on straight away. We went out for two weeks beforehand. It was meant so we could get the partying out of our system but we just carried on through. It was a mental experience, the best times of my life.'

The sight of the pair partying early into the morning was to be a regular one. 'He's got so much stamina,' said Mellor today. Of course, the partying and shooting all night, sleeping all day caused its problems, mainly that Danny was as pale as the day he turned up. Not good news for the producers, who wanted him tanned. 'He had to get fake-tanned up. I remember him getting stark naked and getting fake tan put on,' said Mellor with a laugh.

The two bonded – one, because of the fact that they were young, twenty-year-old lads up for a good time. The other was that on an island packed with British partygoers

– who knew Danny as *Human Traffic*'s Moff and Mellor from *Two Pints of Lager and a Packet of Crisps* – they were quickly seized upon by fans.

'I've got a lot of time for him,' said Mellor. 'He's just so funny. He gets more and more like a parody every time I see him. But he is a very genuine guy.'

However, while Danny certainly revelled in the environment, he looks back at the film now as a completely missed opportunity today. 'One that I watch and cringe at now is *Is Harry on the Boat?* I get a lot of people who come up to me in the street and love it,' he said, during a Q & A with his fans on his website. 'But I was terrible in it. It was a two-bob script and I'm not being arrogant or nothing like that but I was surrounded by two-bob soap stars. Daniela's sweet and all that and Will's all right, but it was one of those jobs. And I was a nutty lunatic at that time. I weighed around four stone in it. I just didn't concentrate on what I was meant to do. It was my first lead role and I didn't do fucking ten per cent of what I can do. It's horrible to watch.'

Although Danny didn't know it, his next film was going to change his life. It would take three more years to come to fruition but *Goodbye Charlie Bright* was a hugely important film for Danny as it introduced him to a new filmmaker – Nick Love. Of course, Danny wasn't to know then that their collaboration would be a constant fixture in British cinemas.

Shot in 1999 under the name *Strong Boys*, the feature debut was a wonderfully shot and vibrant tale of four teenage boys living on a council estate. While the setting was incredibly British, Love was keen not to make a kitchen-sink drama. Although he was a huge fan of Mike Leigh and Alan Clarke's films, he was also a big admirer of Martin Scorsese's innovative camera work, so, despite the setting of a 'crack-den, nasty, kind of nightmarish, council-estate film' (according to the film's producer Charles Steel), it is, in fact, a brightly coloured, sun-soaked, raucous coming-of-age tale.

Dyer plays Francis, a young man who has drifted away from his childhood friends, preferring to spend his time with his girlfriend. He's a sensitive lad, miles away from the Tommy Johnsons and Moffs. He is blindly in love and overjoyed to learn that he is going to be a parent. However, Francis meets a sticky end after crossing paths with the estate's nutter (played by Phil Daniels).

Elsewhere, drawing on his youth, Nick Love's tale is a searing one, which focuses on a group of teenagers during a sweaty summer in a South East London council estate. It tells the exploits of Charlie Bright and his livewire best pal Justin (Roland Manookian). Despite everyone telling Charlie that Justin is keeping him down and that he can do better, he continues to persevere with his best pal despite their difficulties. However, following Francis's death and the dramatic aftermath, Charlie leaves the council estate. When asked by one of the young kids where he is going, Charlie replies, 'Somewhere.'

The film is similar to Scorsese's 1973 breakout hit *Mean Streets*. It's a fantastically enjoyable film and showcased Love as definitely one to watch. While some feel he has not gone on to fulfil the potential of his

Above: Raggle-taggle gypsy Danny Dyer in Cadfael's 'The Leper of St Giles'.

© *Rex Features*

Below: *Children's Ward* in 1995 featured a cherubic Danny (top row, far left).

© *Rex Features*

John Simm, Nicola Reynolds and Danny at the premiere of *Human Traffic*.

Red carpet all the way for Tamar Hassan and Danny.

© Getty Images

Danny with Vinnie Jones for *Mean Machine* in 2001.

Charity football action with *EastEnders'* star Michael Greco. © *Getty Images*

Danny with his partner Jo, his daughter Dani and friend. *© Getty Images*

Mr Danny Dyer.

© *Rex Features*

Ray Winstone and number-one fan Danny Dyer appeared in *All in the Game* on Channel 4.

© *Getty Images*

debut, he has constantly plundered the cast from *Goodbye Charlie Bright* for his later films, including Jamie Foreman, Manookian, Frank Harper and, of course, Danny.

Talking about his young cast, Love acknowledged, 'I consider them the future Brit Pack of working-class actors.'

For *Goodbye Charlie Bright*, Danny was reunited with his *Trench* co-star Nicholls. The WWII drama was the reason Danny got the part in the film, as, despite not thinking *The Trench* worked as a whole, Love thought the chemistry between the pair was perfect for the film.

Costing £2.5 million to make and shot in just seven weeks, the film's day and night shooting took its toll on the estate's residents – and not even the sight of a naked Paul Nicholls streaking in daylight would appease them!

It was well received by the critics, with the *Sun* calling it an 'awesome roller-coaster ride you won't want to get off'. *Time Out* labelled it a 'promising debut' and *Observer* hailed 'a new talent here', while the *Guardian* lauded it for its 'pace, vibrancy and authenticity'. The *Guardian* review is no doubt met with a wry smile from Nick and Danny, as their subsequent outings have been met with vitriol from the newspapers – one of the journalists even wrote a long article, TEN REASONS WHY I HATED OUTLAW, a future Love/Dyer collaboration.

Danny then starred in *High Heels and Low Lifes*. Like *Greenfingers*, it was another charming British comedy. Directed by Mel Smith, it starred Minnie Driver and Mary McCormack as two women who decide to blackmail a couple of bank robbers (Michael Gambon and Kevin McNally) after they overhear them celebrating their latest crime spree. Like Robin Hood, but more glamorous looking, they want to do good with the money. In this case, they supply a local hospital where Driver's character works with expensive medical equipment that they sorely need.

It's a breezy enough affair, with some smart quips. When Driver's character Shannon tells McCormack's Frances that the bank robbers would never allow themselves to be blackmailed by women, Frances replies, 'Why not? It's the twenty-first century. Women are doing every kind of job. We can do extortion.'

Next up in 2001 was *Mean Machine*, an adaptation of the 1974 Hollywood movie, which starred Burt Reynolds. The British version has a significant makeover during the transatlantic flight. Instead of a convict organising a game of American football between the prisoners and prison guards, this time it was football – or soccer to the Americans.

Vinnie Jones stars as Danny Meehan, a former golden boy of English football who shamed the nation when he became involved in match fixing in an England vs Germany game. He is sentenced to Longmarsh prison after drunkenly assaulting two prison officers.

Seeing as he threw a game against England's biggest rivals, he is given a less than warm welcome by both the convicts and the prison guards – most notably a sneering, sadistic Geoff Bell as Ratchett, who would go on to star, memorably so, in *The Business* alongside Danny.

Eager not to annoy his new jailmates even further, he

turns down the chance to coach the prison guards' football team. Instead, he comes up with the idea of organising a 'friendly' between the guards' team and the convicts.

Danny plays Billy the Limpet, a likeable con and a huge football fan. Infatuated with a genuine footballing icon in the same prison, Billy is desperate to prove himself to his idol. There is only one small problem – he's not very good at football. At all. His second-half substitute appearance and subsequent sub-par performance is marked by the Madness song 'Baggy Trousers'.

But he has a big heart and gets to be the inexplicable hero at the end when he nets the last-minute winner, wheeling away in delight with a shirt over his head.

However, he wouldn't go on to steal the film like he did with *Human Traffic* in a supporting role – that honour belonged to Jason Statham's The Monk, a homicidal maniac who is recruited to be the team's goalkeeper.

The film's main fault lies in its overestimation of Jones, not so much as an actor but in his appearance. The hardman Welsh footballer is frequently referred to as a 'pretty boy' by the convicts (and not ironically so either!) and he even proves too appealing to the one female in the prison (Sally Phillips) who is attracted to him almost instantly.

Although not a Guy Ritchie-directed movie, it was produced by Ritchie's producer of choice Matthew Vaughn (now a successful director) and featured several *Lock Stock and Two Smoking Barrels* actors, including Jones, Jason Flemyng and Jason Statham. While he would be reunited with his *Greenfingers* co-stars Adam Fogerty, playing, once again, a dumb criminal and prison-convict lifer David Kelly with a fine line in sage advice, Danny wasn't in the Guy Ritchie gang and he knew it.

It's strange that Danny has never swum in the Guy Ritchie pool of cockney gangster movies. Danny thought he had finally got his chance when he was asked to audition for Ritchie's 2008 film *RocknRolla*. However, it didn't work out as planned.

Danny remembered, 'I read the script and went and met with Guy about it, even though as soon as I walked in the room he said, "There's nothing in it for you." I thought, Well, what the fuck am I here for then?' But we had a nice chat and he said he just wanted to meet me and touch base. I wish him all the best with it. I've got very good friends in it but what's annoying is that reviews of it bring my name up and say, "What the film needs is Danny Dyer."'

It was becoming a difficult time for Danny. It was now two years after his scene-stealing performance in *Human Traffic* and he had yet to find his breakthrough performance. He was still the quirky supporting actor and that didn't look like changing.

The next three years were to be an incredibly lean period. There were roles in TV shows like *Dead Casual*, *Foyle's War*, *Serious and Organised* and *Free Speech*, and he even managed to pop up in virtual form in the two *Grand Theft Auto* games – 2002's *Vice City* and *San Andreas* in 2004. He plays a cockney called Kent Paul. In the second game he is joined by a Mancunian called Maccer – a washed-up musician who is planning a major comeback tour – voiced by none other than Happy Mondays' singer Shaun Ryder.

Just as Danny had to defend the pill-popping antics in *Human Traffic*, and accusations of glorifying football hooliganism in *Football Factory* and vigilantes in *Outlaw*, he had to go on the back foot for his work in the *Grand Theft Auto* series. When asked by the *Metro* in 2007 if they encourage kids 'to go out and nick cars', he replied, 'No. If you're a bit of a nutter and you've got it in your genes, you're going to be like that anyway – watching a film or playing a game isn't going to make any difference. I think they are great games – very clever. I'm proud to be part of them.'

TV series and video-game appearances aside, the reason for the lean period was that Danny seemed to care more about his image off camera than on camera. But that would soon have to change if he wanted to continue as an actor.

Chapter Seven

In the Spotlight

*You strive for fame and success but once you get it
there's no way back*

oday, Danny is quick to swerve the media unless it
suits him. 'I will do the chat-show thing if I've got a
film to promote. I don't want to do it for the sake of it.
It frightens me, the newspapers thing, and I do want to
stay away from that. It's about people respecting me as
an actor, nothing else,' he said. 'That's what's important
to me. I don't want to be in the paper because I've had a
new haircut.'

He also went on to explain why he did the British game
show *Mr & Mrs* in 2008. For someone who is now very
private, it must have come as a shock for his fans to see
him and his fiancée Joanne Mas try to win money for
charity by divulging private details about each other. The
series, which began on British TV in the 1960s, saw
ordinary couples pitted against each other, with the aim of
the game to see which couple knew the most about each
other by answering personal questions. It was axed in the

late 1990s but in 2008 it was revived and rejigged for a new, modern audience. Called *All Star Mr & Mrs* and presented by daytime television royalty Phillip Schofield and Fern Britton, the show would now feature celebrity guests and their partners.

'I got a naughty tax bill, that's why I did *Mr & Mrs*,' explained Danny on his official website. 'I didn't think I would ever go down that route. A weird experience because it's something I don't really want to do.'

Of course, that was Danny speaking today. In the early 2000s, however, there was a completely different story.

After years paying his dues, Danny was now famous. It was something he wanted but even he was shocked at what fame actually entailed. Of course, it didn't help that he was famous for playing a hard-partying pill head.

He told *Little White Lies* in 2007, 'After *Human Traffic* I'd just get cunts who'd give me drugs. One line of coke with me and they'd be happy and on their way. It's weird to think, Do you let them down? Do you say "No"? You have this responsibility.'

He explained further in an interview with *Attitude* magazine, 'A lot of people want to take drugs with me. I will have people come up to me in a fucking packed nightclub with a wrap of gear [cocaine] and a credit card. Instead of asking for an autograph, they are like, "Can I share a line with you?" I try to turn them down and it's hard work. So I snort it and let them go on their way. It's not ideal but that's where fame has got me. It's about being a bad boy and being naughty. And a story about me in the newspaper for sniffing cocaine or smoking a joint is not really a story because I am known as being a fucking bad boy.'

It would be something that Danny would struggle with constantly and is a telling sign of his contradictory nature – the exhibitionist who can't handle the attention.

'You strive for fame and success but once you get it there's no way back. You can't say, "I was wrong. I don't want it any more." Now everywhere I go it seems like people know who I am. And it can be quite frightening.

'I've got a weird audience too. You've got your hippy *Human Traffic* buzzcats. Or the violent *Football Factory* lot, the geezers with scars down their face, a real working-class audience, which I love. But they can be quite dangerous.

'Some days fame is good for my ego. Other days it just pisses me off. I might turn into a hermit soon.

'It's a weird one, fame. For instance, if people knew what I was about and met me and I'm going to go [in a posh English voice], "Hello, my name is Daniel," they'll be fucking devastated. Because they expect a certain thing from me. That's what fame is. If you don't give it to them, they'll be disappointed. So what do you do – do you play up to it or do you be yourself? It's about getting that balance. It's an odd thing to do. Sometimes when people come up to me, I want to go, "Mate, fuck off, you're driving me mad," but I still can't bring myself to do that yet. If someone asks me for a picture or a photo, I'll do it. I've seen other actors who fucking go, "No, no photos," and all this, and you think, What you doing in this game, mate? It's about respecting the people who go to watch your films and respect what you're doing.'

But, after his *Human Traffic* success, fame was new to him and, while it was going to be a rude awakening, he was like a kid in a candy store. Moff had brought him a legion of admirers, including celebrities. 'I was caught up in it, of course I was. Back then, I was living the dream. If celebrity girls wanted to take a bit of interest, that was fine.'

They included *Doctor Who* star Billie Piper, with whom he had a brief relationship. Born in 1982, the singer was fifteen when she burst into superstardom with the catchy pop song 'Because We Want To'. However, fame was something Piper, like Danny, would find hard to deal with. She became more and more estranged from her parents. 'I had very bad phone etiquette,' she says. 'Mostly it was because I wanted to punish them. I wanted them to just be my parents and talk about things that weren't related to what people were saying about me. Now I feel awful about some of the things I said.'

And she suffered from body issues. 'I think it was because I saw so many grown-ups living destructive lifestyles, maybe skipping breakfast, drinking copious amounts of coffee and Diet Coke, smoking fags and being slim and desirable and successful.

'I know that what I go through now is no worse than what my best friends go through who have a relatively healthy relationship with food. Everyone's fucked these days, aren't they? Men too. I mean, men who talk about food endlessly – it's so depressing,' said Piper in a 2008 *Observer* interview.

The pair also remained friends after their split. But

despite their closeness it was still a huge shock for Danny when he found out that Billie had married Chris Evans in 2001. He remembered talking to the then successful pop singer when Evans famously splashed out on a £100,000 Ferrari in a bid to win her heart. 'One day Evans bought her a Ferrari, just left it sitting outside. She was like, "I don't know what to make of it." I said, "Do you fancy him?" She was like, "No, he's ginger and he's got a hairy back." And then she married him.'

He added, in the interview with *Zoo* magazine, 'Don't get me wrong, if it was for real, if someone bought me a Ferrari, I'd give them a chance as well.'

Piper, however, was quick to hit back at the critics. 'People seem to consider that I had a serious meltdown. I married an older man and got pissed in my pyjamas for two years. But these were important formative years for me. Just to relax and care about things that weren't related to what I was doing before. Even though he did help me, it's not as if we were spending all our time talking about our problems and then going out and getting wrecked.' She burst out laughing. 'We were just going out and getting wrecked.'

Danny and Piper became closer following her split from Chris Evans in 2004. The *People* reported that a friend of Billie's told them, 'Danny told Billie he was there for her if she needed him. Billie has very few close friends she can confide in. She needs to talk through her problems with someone she can trust 100 per cent and Danny is that person. They have a very close bond.'

The *Sunday Mirror* also claimed that she poured her

heart out in long phone calls to actor Danny while he was filming *The Business*. An on-set source revealed to the paper, 'Danny's been speaking to Billie a lot. Ever since they went out together a bit, they've remained friends. Obviously, when Billie met Chris she spent a lot less time speaking to him. She was in love with Chris . But now Billie is single again, she and Danny are catching up on old times.'

However, the pair denied any rekindling of their romance. Talking about their brief 2001 romance, Danny said, 'Me and Billie did have a little thing going but it was really low-key. We were more just close friends more than anything else.'

Then there was his fiery two-year engagement with Davinia Taylor. It was during filming of *Is Harry on the Boat?* that he met the *Hollyoaks* beauty and society diva. Danny was not the first celebrity Davinia has dated. In the past she has been linked with Ryan Giggs and Kylie Minogue's ex James Gooding, and she is now married to Premiership footballer Danny Murphy.

Mellor, who had previously worked with Taylor on *Hollyoaks*, was not surprised that the two got together while filming *Is Harry on the Boat?*, as he saw straight away how the pair instantly clicked. He said, 'You knew they were going to get on. They're both party heads. They're both nuts. I have a lot of time for them. You knew what was going to happen.'

Mellor also revealed that a memorable scene in the film, which saw Taylor shock a club rep by appearing with a strap-on dildo, resulted in tears of laughter from the crew when Danny appeared from behind the camera to shout, 'You had better keep that!'

'I don't know if she did,' Mellor added. 'At the end of the day Davinia loves to party. They're the kind of guys you want to be with on a night out.'

And there were plenty of nights out. Their relationship was a tempestuous one and one that the gossip pages loved.

Not that Danny and Davinia seemed to mind. Living in Noel Gallagher's £1.2 million old house, which the Oasis star famously named Supernova Heights, they were perfect media cannon fodder, and it was a regular sight to see the pair coming out of clubs.

But one night saw the pair being named in court – not that they had done anything wrong. Footballers John Terry (who would later become England captain), Jody Morris and Des Byrne were put in the dock for an alleged fracas with bouncer Trevor Thirlwall at one of the hottest, most exclusive nightclubs at the time – The Wellington in Knightsbridge. Run by West End club supremo Jake Panayiotou, the club's clientele read like a who's who of some of the biggest celebrities in the world, including Gwyneth Paltrow, Jude Law, Kate Moss, Mick Jagger and Bono. While the footballers were allegedly getting more drunk, with barman Tom Sherwood remembering that they were downing cocktail after cocktail, Danny Dyer and Davinia Taylor made their entrance.

Terry, being a big fan of Danny's, asked him for an autograph. Danny complied, but as soon as he walked away

Terry threw it away in disgust, much to the amusement of his mates. Des recalled in court that he thought it was funny because 'he should have been asking for John's autograph'. (Terry and Morris were subsequently cleared of all charges, while Byrne was found guilty of possessing an offensive weapon and fined £2,000.)

Danny and Davinia split up soon after but they were still in the media spotlight for months afterwards with rumours that they were back together. One source told the *Daily Mirror* in October 2002, 'Davinia raised eyebrows when she waltzed into the pub with Danny. Everyone thought they were history after splitting up in May. Since then Davinia has said she didn't need anything serious and just wants to have fun but she looked very serious with Danny. Davinia was flirting and giggling.'

But it was clear that it all got too much for Danny. 'It was a part of my life that was quite surreal and not a good time. I was going through a dark place. I hate that whole celebrity side of the business. With Davinia it was all about the clubbing and getting photographed outside places. I could never get my head around it.'

Bizarrely enough, Danny was in an Oscar-winning film during this lean period. Andrea Arnold's *Wasp* won the best short award at the 2005 Academy Awards. It tells the story of Zoe (Natalie Press), a single mother of four hiding the fact she has kids as she embarks on her first date in years. Set on a grim and gritty council estate in Dartford, its ambivalent attitude to a mum leaving her children outside a pub while she goes out on a date with Dave (Dyer) can be seen as a gutsy one.

Explaining where the story idea came from, Arnold said, 'The image that sparked the film was that of a wasp crawling into a baby's mouth. But I just start with an image I can't shake off, work outwards from that and see what comes out.'

In her Oscar speech, Arnold, a former children's-TV presenter, said, 'This is truly overwhelming. I'm not really used to this kind of thing. I'd like to thank everyone who worked on the film, everyone who worked at the studio really hard – they know who they are. The beers are on me when I get home. What can I say? In England I'd say that this is the dog's bollocks. Thank you very much.'

And Danny, delighted with the Oscar win, was quick to brag that he'd won an Academy Award before Mirren. Talking in 2007, he said, 'She [Mirren] is fucking great. I got my Oscar before her. I got one in 2005 for *Wasp*, a short film I did. I guess it rubbed off on her.'

Arnold would go on to direct the critically acclaimed *Red Road* in 2006 – a Scottish thriller that focuses on a female CCTV security operator who spots a man from her past. While Natalie Press featured in the movie, there was no room for Danny. A shame, as Danny puts in a sterling performance in *Wasp* and it would have been interesting to see what Arnold could have done with Danny on a feature-length movie.

And so it seemed the offers were drying up. While he was putting on a brave face – 'The one thing I do love about this job is nothing's set out. You don't know what might be around the corner. It might be fuck all. I might get no fucking work' – he was becoming more and more disillusioned.

He was turning up to auditions drunk, waltzing on to the set with a bottle of vodka in his hand. 'I was getting work at the time,' recalled Danny. 'But I'd get picked up at 7am and go in after a mad session, thinking everyone loved me. But that doesn't work in such a small industry. I was surrounded by coke heads and I've had to cut them off a bit. People were chucking pills at me left, right and centre. I'd swallow them, whereas now I go, "Nope."'

If it represented the darkest period in Danny's life, it is also one that has served him so well. It made him realise what he didn't want. He wanted to be known for his work rather than for who was draped over his arms coming out of a nightclub.

'My family is now the most important thing in the world. These days I don't want to wake up at 4pm with a massive hangover and wonder where my life has gone.'

He wanted to make a film that would encourage debate and attract a cult and devoted audience – in short, films that would make a difference. But who would hire him? With his lifestyle seemingly taking precedence over his films and his head not in the right place, it would take a brave man to sign him for such a movie – and an even crazier one if he was to put Danny in the lead.

Enter Nick Love.

Chapter Eight

It's a Funny Old Game

We're living in a naughty world; let's make a film about it

'There's nothing different about me. I'm just another bored male, approaching thirty, in a dead-end job, who lives for the weekend – casual sex, watered-down lager, heavily cut drugs and occasionally kicking the fuck out of someone.'

So goes the opening monologue by Danny's character in 2004's *The Football Factory*. And, accompanied by incendiary footage of stills shots of police troubles, newspaper clippings of football violence, CCTV footage of the actors walking in side streets, police helicopters flying around to a high-octane soundtrack, it makes for a searing intro.

His opening speech is almost trumped by one that follows soon after. 'What else you going to do on a Saturday? Sitting in your armchair, fucking wanking off to *Pop Idol*, then trying to avoid your wife's gaze as you struggle to come to terms with your sexless marriage, then go spunk your wages on kebabs, fruit machines and brasses. Fuck that for a laugh. I know what I would rather do. Tottenham away. Love it.'

With dialogue like this, and delivered with roguish intensity, it's no surprise that Tommy Johnson has become one of Danny's most revered and well-known characters by his fans. From Johnson's opening swagger (which incidentally was added as a reshoot to show who the film's star was at the beginning), he was the character of a lifetime for Danny. And boy did he know it.

Speaking to *AXM* magazine, he said, 'I think there's not been a film made like this in a long time, something so controversial. Whether you like the film or not, it has an impact. You come out of there thinking, Fucking hell! That's what I like – a bit of controversy. I don't want to do the run-of-the-mill, cheese-on-toast fucking boring shit. I like to do something that's a bit out there and a bit fucking mad.'

Based on the book by John King about the notorious football firm the Chelsea Headhunters, which *Trainspotting* author Irvine Welsh described as 'the best book I have ever read about football and working-class culture in the 1990s', it follows the exploits of young football hooligan Tommy Johnson and his weekend pastime of 'kicking the fuck out of someone'. After he begins suffering from a series of violent dreams that suggest he is going to get brutally beaten up, he begins to wonder if he should pursue a life away from hooliganism.

The film was due to be made earlier, without Nick Love's involvement, and, funnily enough, Danny was handed a chance to audition for it. Disappointingly, he had been turned down, but he was given a second chance thanks to Love.

Danny seized on the role with glee. The normal working-class twenty-something with a love for booze and pulling girls on a Saturday night was a role that fitted Danny like a glove. He was able to draw on real-life experience from his time on the terraces with his father at Upton Park during the 1980s, which was rampant with hooliganism.

Speaking in 2004, he explained, 'I don't see [the] point in it myself but people take it passionately. It's more about the territory – it's not really about the football at all. There's a handful of people and it's all about the area and where they come from. I don't really get it, to be honest with you, but it happens and this film is based on facts. I see it going on around me but I prefer to swerve it. I'm an actor, not a fighter.'

He also realised, though, that there was more to Johnson than just being a thug. The greatest difficulty was making him likeable.

'It was important to me that I put that across. You really need to care about Tommy by the end of the film. You have to make him endearing, even though he's running about swearing and being violent. There's also this underlying thing where he is quite sensitive and is thinking about things.'

Like Danny, Tamer Hassan seized on the chance to star in *The Football Factory*. He was given the standout part of the head of the Millwall firm, the notorious Bushwackers.

And, like many of the cast and director, the Millwall fan didn't find it hard to find to get into character. 'At the end of the day, I've owned nightclubs, restaurants and have come across real thugs. I used to go to football with the main boys from Millwall,' he told the BBC. 'For me, research wasn't an issue.'

However, he added in an interview with the *Guardian*, 'I've never been a Millwall hooligan, so acting one wasn't something I was overjoyed to do. But to play anything to do with Millwall was fantastic for me.'

Another standout in the film was the bitter Billy Bright, played with delightfully resentful menace by Frank Harper. A schoolground bully who never grew up, he's a man mountain fuelled by seething jealousy and childlike pettiness, despite having a successful floristry business, a loving wife and kids, and a nice home.

To the credit of Love's casting, Harper also didn't have to look far for inspiration. 'I've been around people like that all my life. It was just part and parcel of where I grew up. I've never been involved in football violence – my dad would have disowned me. And I'm one of a lucky minority that has found an outlet in the arts. But there are generations out there who feel really lost – and they are the most un-PC group in the country: white, working-class heterosexuals. The people New Labour hate. They feel they've got no place in their own country any more. And they are expressing their frustration through drinking and violence.'

Love himself was able to draw on real-life experiences. 'I've seen what goes on. Personally, I don't have that propensity for violence. But I've been out with my mates on "manoeuvres", as they call them. And it's fucking terrifying.

'I've got lots of mates who are football thugs or have been football thugs and they don't moralise about it. The bottom line is they do it because they enjoy the buzz. It's not about any deep, endemic social issues: football thugs come from all different walks of life.'

Love was such a fan of the book that he tried to buy the rights soon after its release in 1997. 'I just thought it was a very under-represented cultural phenomenon. It's the kind of thing that has gone on in England since the 1970s.' However, he lost out on the rights in a bidding auction to film company Vertigo Films and thought that was the end of that, especially considering that in November 2002 the cameras began to roll on the adaptation. 'I'd wanted to option the book myself in 1998 but I couldn't afford it. I knew I was the man to do it and John King too.'

Luckily, both were to get that wish, as the original project, which would have featured Sean Bean and Dougray Scott, didn't last long because of unspecified problems and Love was to be reacquainted with his pet project shortly afterwards.

Vertigo Films were desperate to get Love on board. But he was adamant that they scrap their script so he could start from scratch. And because Love was so passionate about the project, and because the story he wanted to tell had been floating around his head for years, he managed to hand in the script in only four days. 'The script far exceeded what we had expected from a first draft; this contained all the elements of how we envisaged the film being brought to the big screen,' said producer James Richardson.

Love also insisted of handpicking his cast and crew. *Goodbye Charlie Bright*'s Jamie Foreman, Roland Manookian and Frank Harper all returned, as did Danny in a bigger role this time. Even before he had finished the script, he knew he wanted Danny as Tommy Johnson – something Danny was naturally delighted about. (Tamer Hassan was also cast before the script was finished.) Love commented, 'These two were in it before they auditioned. I think, if you are making a film about a subject like this, which has to be absolutely believable, you can only cast people who aren't football thugs – Danny and Tamer aren't football thugs but they have a real understanding about male culture, tribalism and hierarchy. They have such gravitas as actors. For years, these sorts of films weren't getting made. It's quite hard to act and be natural but you have these parts that are almost written for you, you can really be yourself in it.'

Rounding off the cast was Neil Maskell as Rod – who described the shoot as 'a bunch of mates hanging out, having a brilliant experience on set' – and veteran actor Dudley Sutton as Bill Farrell – who said yes without reading the script, as he was so impressed with what Love had to say. 'Nick Love called me up and said, "I want you to do my next film," and I said, "Yes" straight away because I have a lot of trust and respect for him. He is lovely to work with, straight talking and very honest.'

Shot over six weeks during April and May 2003 in

South East London, it was financed by Vertigo Films and produced by James Richardson and a certain Allan Niblo – the producer on *Human Traffic*.

There was to be no controversy this time around. Niblo was attracted to the film as soon as he read the book, which was handed to him by actor Steve North, an associate producer on the film, who also starred in The Brighton Theatre Company's 1998 stage version of *The Football Factory*.

'After reading *The Football Factory*, I knew it was vital to turn it into a feature film, both from a cultural and cinematic point of view,' said Niblo. 'The book captures football culture's underbelly better than any fiction I have come across. To portray this, we needed to find a director who not only knew the background to the book but also understood how to translate the story to the big screen.'

What drove Love on was that, although the subject of football hooliganism has been tackled in books, documentaries and plays ever since a *Panorama* programme gave us an inside look at Millwall's hooligans in the 1970s, apart from the 1980s muddled effort *ID*, the subject had never really been tackled on screen.

'Previous films about football violence have never worked because of the lack of attention to detail, the implausibility of the characters and the ridiculous way that the actual violence is handled,' he said in an interview with the *Telegraph* in 2006. 'And there's nothing worse than watching a film and thinking, I don't believe this. So we roped in thugs from most of the London "firms" – though we were terrified of local rivalries spilling over into actual fighting. But the astonishing thing was, at the end of take, they all started clapping and bowing to each other.'

Danny himself was certainly getting stuck in. When Danny's character got violently beaten up in the tunnel, he ended up getting a smack in the face for real by his co-star Daniel Naylor. 'I'm the bloke who hit Danny. It don't feel good as me and him are going to have to share a car on the way home. It was a good punch anyway,' he said on set.

Danny recalled, 'Fucking hell, I caught a couple of digs on the chin. Couple of boots but I took it in my fucking stride.'

The final riot scene was incredibly hard to prepare and was a meticulously planned affair. It was a scene that scared Nick the most from day one. He had never done anything on this scale before and it was a fear that plagued him throughout.

'The lead up to shooting the big fight was tremendously nerve wracking as we didn't know if the fights would get out of hand. There were rumours that we'd get bombarded by real firms,' recalled Love. 'Thankfully, this didn't happen. We had achieved a seemingly impossible task of capturing a realistic fight between rivals Millwall and Chelsea without incident. The last week was the biggest elation from the crew and cast. Everything had the potential to go very wrong. There was also a press photographer lurking in the bushes, taking sneaky photos. It was a mad day but everything worked out very well. After that day we all thought, Fuck it, we've done it.

'The best day for me was the Chelsea vs Millwall fight. So many people were involved and the adrenalin rush was amazing. It was like being back in the playground, only with grown-ups. It was like a scene out of *Braveheart*,' recalled Danny.

But Hassan revealed in a 2007 interview that he had reservations about the fight scene because the extras were so young. 'The hardest thing was this melee at the end. You know, I turned up on set and there was like what I can only say were youngsters with baseball bats and wearing Burberry [gear]. I said, "Listen, I'm not going into battle with these kids," and they sort of started going, "Look, Tam, it's just a film." I said, "But this is a way of life for people. I'm representing a culture here and I live in this area, and if we are to portray this in the right way, I will need to go into battle with some real people." So they said, "OK, we understand you but where will we get such people?" So I got on the phone to a couple of people and they got all the right boys down.

'Can you picture this? You've got sixty non-actors behind you and you're at the helm, and you've got to lead these into battle. I mean, I wished Nurofen sponsored that day because it was the hardest day's work I had to ever do. It was so challenging and we got a few digs; I got a few punches in the mouth, a few cuts and bruises for the cause, which, for me, that's the hardest day's work I've ever had to have.'

Love was desperate to do this film, not only because he is a huge football fan (he has 'Millwall' inked in blue on the inside of his lip and another tattoo on his foot) but also because the story was a compelling one – less about football (indeed, the game itself is only featured in one scene), more about the arrested development of the male psyche.

'One of the themes of the movie is about armies. Men who have either been in armies or who are looking for armies. The young men looking to be in an army, while the old man has been in the army – with young men thinking war is cool. It's about older generations clashing with the young generation.

'The potential leader Tommy Johnson is in his twenties, Billy Bright is in his forties, with a tendency to use his fists. Zeberdee is in his late teens, representing a new breed of evil, and finally there is Bill Farrell in his seventies, who has fought for his country during WWII but doesn't believe in violence,' he said in the film's production notes.

And Love was keen to point out that the nearly twenty per cent rise in the number of arrests at football matches that year was down to the time's popular drug of choice. He told theage.com, 'You don't have to be a brain surgeon to realise that drugs change cultures. Cocaine has become the drug of choice for the working-class man. In the 1980s it was always speed and alcohol, which was why people were always fighting. Then ecstasy came along and nobody could be bothered to fight – they just wanted to dance in fields. Now England is just swamped in cocaine – it's like a white blanket over London. Blokes like to have a bit of gear as a sharpener and have a couple of drinks to go with it, then bang: you're hyped up, ready to go to war.'

He added, in an interview with Will Self, 'I'm against it but I ask myself, if a hundred men want to get together, with no innocent bystanders or police involved, and beat the shit out of each other, why shouldn't they be allowed to?'

Sensing that the film's subject matter could cause controversy, especially when Love was giving away quotes like that for free, the film's producer James Richardson tried to placate the media. 'It's very real and we show what happens,' he said. 'It's very ugly and messy, and not much fun. It proves a big adrenaline rush for some but there is a price to pay and we want to show both sides. We are not taking a moral stance but we are putting the issue out there. We want to create a seminal film; what *Trainspotting* did for the drugs culture, we want to do for hooligans.

'The film is about a bunch of friends, their relationship and the world they live in. Everyone thinks hooliganism has gone underground but that's not the case. There have been some major set-piece fights in the last few months. It's never gone away and we're raising the debate.'

And debate was something that was indeed being raised. If all publicity is good publicity, *The Football Factory* was having the time of its life. Something the English FA were all too aware of. 'We don't want to give *The Football Factory* any more publicity than it is getting,' was their official comment.

The film was quickly criticised by the media and MPs – who accused the film of glorifying football violence in the wake of that year's summer football tournament Euro 2004. Because of England's association with hooliganism in the 1970s and 1980s, every two years (be it the European Championship or the World Cup) the subject rears its ugly head. If England ever did get expelled from the tournament in Portugal, as had been threatened if English fans should revert to their ugly ways, it would have surely been a catastrophe for the country. UEFA dealt the warning to the FA after small sections of fan trouble during Euro 2000 and the World Cup in France in 1998. So it was unsurprising that government officials were wary of the film's release so close to the tournament. Simon Hughes, Liberal Democrat MP for North Southwark and Bermondsey, which includes the Millwall area, led the criticism, saying, 'It's irresponsible for the film to be shown so close to the event and it will give ammunition to the people who are anti-football and anti-England.'

His views were echoed by 2004's Shadow Culture Media and Sport Secretary Julie Kirkbride. 'The timing could not be worse. It's grossly irresponsible for the filmmakers to glorify this type of mindless violence and to make a profit out of wholly unacceptable behaviour.'

Millwall's then manager Dennis Wise even went as far as banning his players from the premiere of the film. A spokesperson for the club said, 'It's regrettable for a film that casts football and football supporters in a negative light to be appearing on the eve of the biggest game in Millwall's history [the FA Cup Final with Manchester United] and shortly before England fans head off to Euro 2004. It is naive to suggest that hooliganism is a thing of the past.'

Indeed, while an increased police presence, a different

football fan base and the added security measures including CCTV cameras, stricter banning orders and all-seater stadiums had ensured that there would be no repeat of the rampant hooliganism of the past, there was an increase in bans imposed from 1,149 to 1,794 and offences rose by thirteen per cent in the 2002/03 season according to Home Office figures.

Love said, 'There is a huge amount of anger and disillusionment among young men that gets its release in football. Anyone who sees this and then goes out and is violent is disturbed anyway. I just don't believe films have the power – I wish they did.'

Danny was unsurprisingly keen to wade into the debate, saying, 'We're going to get that kind of thing because of the timing of the film. Yet the violence has been going on for years. I don't think one film is going to make any difference – if anything it will be a deterrent. We're showing the reality. We're not saying if it's right or wrong, just portraying what goes on.'

Another cast member was forced to call for calm during the subsequent hostility from the media. Love regular Roland Manookian, like his part in *Goodbye Charlie Bright*, plays a young and unpredictable livewire – this time a guy called Zeberdee.

'Because football violence is such a hot potato, it's easy to overlook how balanced the film is,' said Manookian. 'And I don't seriously think that any film has the power to affect English hooliganism one way or another: if people are going to cause trouble at Euro 2004, they'll do it regardless.'

At one point his character racially abuses an Asian man and his son, much to the disgust of the film's moral guide Bill Farrell. The war hero constantly looks on in revulsion on what today's generation is like, and is quick to point out that he fought in the war to stop exactly the sort of fascism that he now sees.

Manookian, who is of Armenian descent and was constantly bullied throughout his youth in Bermondsey, was particularly moved by that scene. 'The older character, Bill, actually fought against far-right extremists in the war, and that point is explicitly made in the film.'

While the media were having a field day with the controversy, ex-football hooligans were quick to come to the support of the movie. 'We had two hundred members of Cardiff City's Soul Crew at a screening and they were made up by the film,' said Love. '*Guardian* and *Independent* readers find it disturbing. It's unashamedly aimed at the people it's about. It's about men who don't want to grow up. For them it's about passion, heroics, the recounting of battles, and it's uniquely British and apparently endlessly fascinating to the rest of the world.'

A former member of the Millwall Bushwackers, who refused to be named, said, 'I can't believe all the fuss it has caused – it's the reality.' Speaking at the film's premiere, he added, 'It's a few people punching each other, it isn't a big deal. We only fight people who want to fight. It's about camaraderie and respect, and friends having a laugh. At the end of the day it's just a film.'

'It's bang on. My hackles went up during the opening scene,' said Andy Link, a former football hooligan with the Leeds United firm Service Crew. 'I stood up, bouncing around. I knew those guys. They were the people I used to see every Saturday. It's a complete addiction. There's nothing that beats the endorphin rush when you're having a row.'

The film was in the news again when a major cinema chain in Stockholm withdrew the film from its chain after a fight between rival fans of Malmo FF and Helsingborg broke out during a screening.

The film's ambiguous ending also stoked the flames of controversy. After Tommy Johnson's premonition comes true and he is left for dead, he finally has the chance to leave that part of his life for good.

Love admits that he was torn by the ending. 'He has been given life-changing possibilities, he has nightmares about being attacked and left for dead, and sees omens of death and violence but we are not sure what he is going to do about it.'

'Was it worth it?' Tommy asks himself in his closing voiceover, before strolling into the pub to the delight of his friends. 'Course it fucking is.'

A controversial ending but one that Nick finally decided to plump for because, in reality, he felt that's what the character would have done. 'Tommy's an unredeeming character,' added Love.

Danny cemented his status as 'one of the people' when he refused to act like the movie star on set. Not that he had much choice when most of the extras were real-life hooligans! 'It's got some proper real lunatics in it. He [Love] didn't want extras in it, poncing about. He wanted people in the background who'd been there and had it off. So I was roaming about with absolute raving lunatics and that helped me. I didn't really get a chance to be an actor on set; I just had to be one of the lads. I couldn't go, "Hold on a moment, I just gotta do my lines." I would have been fucking ruined. I had to just get in with the boys, make sure they liked me and do my lines in my own time.'

He added to *AXM* magazine, 'I just hope the audiences get it. It's not just about lunatics running about, whacking people up, 'cause there's only about ten minutes of real violence in the film, at the beginning and at the end. The rest is the tension of it and that's the genius of it – the tension throughout the film, waiting for the kick-off.'

Danny needn't have worried about being liked or whether audiences would get it. It wasn't long before the cast reaped the rewards from an adoring audience. In fact, Tamer and Danny were stunned when they were constantly being cheered by members of the public and treated like local heroes long before the film had come out. Even the cast hadn't actually seen the film at that point, yet Danny's and Tamer's lines from the movie were being spouted back to them. 'I go on to the terraces in Millwall and I'm like a celebrity,' recalled Tamer.

'The reason for that is an incomplete pirate DVD of the film got out last year and from one DVD it's turned into an epidemic,' explained Love. 'Tens of thousands of copies are going up and down the country. The thing is the pirate is only one tenth of the real film; it's missing voiceover, music and credits. A lot of people have seen the pirate and love it. Part of me wishes I had thought of it myself as it has been a great bit of underground marketing.'

Tamer added, 'How anyone got their hands on a copy I'll never know. I've heard people say, "My mate just printed off five thousand copies," or "I've just bought it off eBay." What they are watching is basically just a rough edit – but people adore it. Everywhere I go, I get stopped in the petrol station, builders will come up to me and say, "You was brilliant, mate. I'm a Millwall supporter and you've done us proud." And I find myself thinking, You've seen it already? I haven't even seen it.'

It is one scene in particular that Tamer finds being constantly repeated back to him. His character, joined by the hoodlums from his firm, are on the lookout for Johnson, although they have no idea what he looks like. When they walk into the toilet where Johnson is and ask him what his name is, he replies with the effeminate moniker 'Dorian'.

'Everybody has picked up on this,' he said in a 2004 interview. 'I'll be standing at the toilet in Millwall and people come up to me saying, "All right, Dorian?" They then start crying with laughter.'

It seems hooliganism was a popular topic, what with rival hooligan film *Green Street*, starring Elijah Wood, coming out a year later.

Danny was quick to scoff. 'Elijah Wood? That film is laughable. I had a little butchers at the script and I thought, This is a joke. I can see what Elijah Wood is doing as an actor – he's trying to get as far away from *The Lord of the Rings* as possible. I just think he's made the wrong decision and I don't think he realises how big the football culture is here. He's not going to get away with it in this country,' he said in a 2004 interview in the *Mirror*. 'Fair play to him for trying it on, but he's going to make himself look like an idiot. I'm just really happy that our film is coming out first, so theirs is going to be compared to it. Ours is untouchable really.'

At the premiere of *The Football Factory*, Danny was even more damning of Wood, ranting, 'He's going to be laughed off the screen. He's a Hobbit and at the end of the day you can't put a Hobbit in a film about hooliganism. He looks about twelve.'

It was a point with some truth. Despite *Nuts* magazine proclaiming it as making '*The Football Factory* look like a girly playground scrap', the film came and went with barely any impact. The only controversy seemed to stem from the fact that West Ham apparently felt conned after giving the filmmakers their blessing to shoot at Upton Park without realising how violent the film would be.

It was an accusation that the film's director Lexi Alexander furiously denied. 'It's an urban myth we scammed them – they are not that stupid. I promised them it would be a film that fundamentally opposed violence and they read part of the script. They were worried when some paparazzi shots came out of the more graphic scenes but, when they saw the final product, they were happy,' she told the *Newham Recorder*.

No matter, because Danny was unsurprisingly quick to put the boot in after watching the film. 'It was a pile of rubbish, absolute shit, which pleased me because they had such a big budget and I would have been gutted it if had been better than *The Football Factory*.'

Hassan said about *Green Street* – 'Without being biased, I think *The Football Factory* is the closest you are going to get to authenticating real situations as to how hooliganism is portrayed today. There were some flaws in *Green Street* and I'm sure everyone who has seen it has said it. But they're just two different films and there's no point in comparing them with each other or any other films.'

And it certainly wasn't looked on fondly by real-life hooligans – unlike *Football Factory*. As for film critics, there was an incredibly mixed bag with reviews ranging from the likes of 'Dyer is superb' (the *Telegraph*) to 'Love does come dangerously close to making it all look like fun' (*The Times*). No matter what the critics thought, this was a film cherished by football fans. It was to be the film that Danny had hoped he would make ever since he got into acting.

Chapter Nine
A Tough Love

We love each other dearly

The *Football Factory* got Danny right back into the nation's heart. And, while he had Nick Love to thank for casting him in the first place, he also owed the director a lot more than just that. Love forced Danny to take a long, hard look at his life and to get his priorities straight. Indeed, he has regularly credited him for 'saving me from a really dark period when I couldn't get any work'.

Love had been impressed with Danny on *Goodbye Charlie Bright* but the actor he worked with on that film was a different one now. 'I was going through a stage of being a bit fucked in the nut. I was turning up for work with bottles of vodka in my hand, just really caning it, and people starting to turn their backs on me in the business. They weren't hiring me because I was a liability,' said Danny.

But Love was desperate to get his man for *The Football Factory*. While there was some initial dissent about Danny's casting, Love had no doubt. He just needed assurance from Danny – and he was determined to let Danny know that this was a big chance and it was his to blow.

Danny explained, 'Nick came up with this and said he really wanted me to be the lead but the producers were worried about me and I was going to have to audition for it. He gave me that kick up the ass. We had a meeting in the Groucho Club and he told me straight. He bollocked me and he was right. I got all choked up, went away and had a real think about it.'

It was a typical case of tough love and it worked a treat. Nick's words hit Danny hard. He remembers going home and crying his eyes out. He knew this was a role of a lifetime and he would be 'devastated if I didn't get the role... He snapped me out of the lull that I was in and I needed that. Few people could've said that to me. It was a real turning point.' Danny happily admits he knew that he had been given a second chance by Love and he was desperate to not throw it away. 'I didn't go on the piss once in six weeks, was getting to bed early, getting up early and really enjoying what I was doing. I needed a job like this to come along as I was on my way out. I had the chance to show everything of what I'm about, the best part of my personality. I'm the lead, I narrate it, and I carry the film.'

Not only did Danny get a breakthrough role but he also gained a best friend in Love.

Love's films have all dealt strongly with male camaraderie. Indeed, his films can be seen as love stories between men, whether it's the tempestuous relationship between Charlie Bright and Justin, Tommy Johnson and his pals, Frankie and The Playboy in *The Business* or the male bonding of the Outlaws. 'Nick's very obsessed with men. He's very interested in men loving each other in a straight way. The way men bully each other and gossip and slag their mates off,' said Danny.

It shouldn't come as a surprise that the pair have struck up a close relationship. Like Danny, Love has the arts – in his case directing – to thank for saving him from a wild life.

Although Love was a 'middle-class boy' and a chess champion at the age of ten, he happened to find himself regularly hanging around the Greenwich council estates, 'running amok' and being a 'horrible little monster'. In fact, it was these adolescent experiences that formed the basis for the storyline of his much-lauded debut *Goodbye Charlie Bright*.

The death of one of his closest friends hit Love hard and he went off the rails. Later he said of that time, 'I'd been kicked out of school when I was fourteen, I didn't have any qualifications, I had no focus, no job, nothing. I was just living day to day. And that was the first time in years when I was able to think, Look, what are you really doing? You're like a leaf being blown around in the wind and you're always going to be this way unless you make some radical changes. I was really fucking fortunate that there were a few people around me, like my mum, who made a really, really concerted effort to break the cycle with me. Fortunately, I was young enough that it could still be broken. But a lot of the kids I grew up with, now they're in prison, they're junkies or they're dead.'

Not that Love doesn't take responsibility for what happened. 'It wasn't like I was getting abused by my father or anything. It was more about me wanting to be a bad boy. You can't admit that at the time, you want to feel like a victim. But I'm old enough and honest enough to say, "You know what? I wanted to be a bad seed and so I was."'

It was only when he happened to come across *The Firm* – a TV movie about football hooliganism – that things began to change. Directed by Alan Clarke, it sparked something fiercely in Love's system and made him realise that the people and the society that Clarke talked about was one that he knew incredibly well.

'It was about my world, my people, and I thought, I can do that, I can tell a story like that.'

He managed to get a job as a runner at a production company, before moving to Bournemouth to study at a film school. 'I was just so lucky to get another chance. And I took that second chance with gusto.'

With a newfound passion he worked his way up through his system. In between that time he worked as a model, when he was twenty, during a year in San Francisco, for Ralph Lauren ('It wasn't my thing at all,' he recalled) and managed to earn £100,000, but 'I wasted it all,' he laughed. There was also his four-month marriage to *EastEnders* actress Patsy Palmer – a relationship that may well have been short but he claims they are still on speaking terms.

Again, as for Danny, *The Football Factory* was a second chance for Love. While *Goodbye Charlie Bright* was ecstatically well received, with the famed late critic Alexander Walker saying, 'Goodbye Charlie Bright shares with Billy Elliot a feeling for the absolute compulsion to escape from the ghetto of environmental pressures or tribal entropy that stifle the best and the brightest. A small film, yes – but unexpectedly, a very good one.'

But, according to Love, it still 'bombed at the box office'. It was a huge blow to Love, who took the film's financial failure to heart. He had poured his heart into the script and was devastated when the critical rave never translated into box-office success.

The years in between the two films saw Love in the directorial wilderness – even taking on a job selling Christmas trees. But he still knew that directing was his life calling. Talking about his memories on his debut, he recalled, 'It seemed like the most natural thing I'd ever done. After all, films are like battles, they're made in the preparation... After I said, "Action!" I never looked back.'

And when he finally got his second chance, just like Danny, he was making sure that he wasn't going to blow it.

Danny saw Love as finally someone in the business who recognised and nurtured the talent that he had. He had found something of a kinship – although it was a complex one – akin to an older brother or father relationship. Love's approval was something that Danny desperately sought, and it was something that Love didn't dish out liberally.

'The thing with Nick is that, when he does compliment

you – which isn't very often – when he does give you a tap on the back, you worship it,' explained Danny. 'He's not a poncy director – he'll tell you fucking straight. If he doesn't like it, he'll tell you you're a cunt. He'll tell you to sort yourself out and I like that about him. Most actors would crumble under Nick Love; they wouldn't be able to deal with him. Our little firm – me, Frank Harper, Tamer Hassan, Roland, Tony Denton, we all know what he's about. We're all from the flats, so that's the way we work, and we work well.'

And, although Danny is an actor that doesn't like to prepare for a role, and is someone who likes to be 'given a blank page and go where I want with it', he feels at home with Love's dialogue.

Like Martin Scorsese/Robert De Niro, Ridley Scott/Russell Crowe or Tim Burton/Johnny Depp – the Dyer/Love collaboration is increasingly becoming a fixture on the big screen. Their working relationship is quite simple. When Nick disappears off the face of the earth for a couple of months without any notice, Danny knows he's working on a script. He'll have no idea what the film will be about or what part he will play – if there is even a part for him. The next time he sees Love he will be handed the finished material.

While promoting 2007's *Outlaw*, Danny revealed, 'He comes back and says, "Here you go, Dan, that's the next one." I didn't have a clue what it was about. I always know when he puts a script in front of me it's going to be special. I just didn't know how special.'

The same year he explained further to *Female First*, 'We

have a great chemistry; we have got a lot of belief in each other. He writes great dialogue that I can just speak so easily, I can bring it to life. [Also] I don't have an ego, I don't really label myself as a movie star and I work for fuck all, which is good news for him. He can just let me get on with my thing. He doesn't have to worry about me, he can go off and do other things, he doesn't need to hug me and tell me how good I am. I just get on with it. He does tweak me now and again though.'

The films that are on Danny's pre-Love CV that he is proud of include the likes of *Loved Up*, *Human Traffic* and *Wasp* – films that say something about the city that he loves, which you don't normally find in a Hugh Grant comedy. And that was something that would be retained with his partnership with Love.

He told *Little White Lies*, 'He likes to make controversial films. He wants people to have a fucking opinion about it, whether they love it or hate it. What he hates is [when] people watch it and go to Pizza Express and just forget about it.'

Love sees Danny as an actor who is 'easy to work with. He may say cunt a lot but he's very down to earth, generous and an easy-going person. He's easy to identify with if you're a working-class man aged between eighteen and thirty – the kind who have traditionally come to see our films. People can relate to him.'

Danny is a little bit more bullish as to why Nick constantly uses him as his leading man. 'I think his dialogue comes out of my mouth better than any other actor,' he told *Film Review* in 2005.

Love is also a highly insecure filmmaker. When this author met him for an interview in 2007, he was quick to put himself down at any opportunity. 'If I knew someone who could direct my scripts I would let them. I'm not that talented,' he said. While seemingly quite harsh, it's not a sole moment of weakness. Interviews and comments on his enjoyable film commentaries are littered with such self-deprecating put-downs. Perhaps Danny's loyalty and reverence means it's one less thing to worry about on the film set.

Certainly, Love is comfortable with his 'regular group' – and given that in *Outlaw*, he ditched many regulars, Danny aside, resulting in some of his worst reviews, he may call on his circle in the future. Danny hopes so anyway, 'We've got our own clique of people, our little firm. That's the genius of Nick. I like to look at it like a *Carry On* vibe; he has a certain group of actors and he swaps the roles around. The great thing for me is that he's kept me as his leading man, he likes me to tell his story, you know. It just rolls off my tongue – he always says it's his brain and my mouth, and it's a great partnership. I look at him as my partner in crime, there's no two ways about that. He's the greatest director I've worked with. We love each other dearly and I love having talent like his around me. He trusts me and I trust him with my life.'

Love has vowed to not be swayed by the Hollywood dollar and insists he will be making more films holding a microscope to British working-class culture for the near future. So despite Danny not featuring in Love's next film

The Firm – the first time Love has made a film without Danny – the pair will no doubt be causing controversy on the big screen once more.

Chapter Ten

Childhood Sweetheart

Jo is the fucking love of my life. She keeps me in check

While he has Nick Love to thank for his career comeback, another person helped Danny get back on the straight and narrow, and his personal life was finally becoming as stable as his career.

He was desperate to turn his back on the constant gossip-column lifestyle that he had become accustomed to. 'When you get a bit famous it's hard to find a bird who's not just after your money,' he said. 'I don't want a bird waiting for me with a crate of beer and a line of coke. You want someone who you can sit down and watch a bit of *EastEnders* with.'

Becoming famous had shown Danny that there were people that weren't as straightforward with their motives as he was. He was becoming cynical, and he wanted something similar to what he had had with his childhood sweetheart and the mother of his child. In fact, it was becoming clear he didn't just want a girl like Joanne, he wanted Joanne.

Because Joanne knew him before he became famous, she wouldn't accept any prima-donna behaviour – an attitude that he found appealing. 'I need someone like her who'll bollock me, not roll over and laugh at everything I say,' he admitted in an interview in 2007.

He told the *Observer*, 'I used to think that the man goes out to work and the woman puts the food on the table, but I don't any more. Those days are gone. Women are powerful. It's a different world. And I quite like that.'

Despite breaking up in their teenage years, they had still remained close, unsurprisingly since they had a child together. But he was tired of going off the rails and sought Joanne for comfort. 'I went through a bit of a wild stage and needed to get everything out of my system. I've grown up a lot through that. Joanne has gone and done her thing as well but we got to a stage of our lives when we weren't with anyone else and thought, do you know what? We're getting on really well. Why don't we just get back together?' he told the *Mirror*, while promoting *The Football Factory*.

For Danny it was the best decision he has ever made, as he knows that the gap in years when they weren't together has actually ensured their long-term future.

'We had a kid very young and didn't know how to deal with it all, being together from such a young age,' he said in 2006. 'We split up a few years ago and basically we needed to sleep with other people. And it worked too. I am so lucky to be with her. When we had split up, we'd still see each other and then we realised we were meant to be.'

Of course, in order to get back with Joanne he had to curb his wild lifestyle. 'I've calmed down. I have a kid so I want to make it work this time,' he said in 2004. 'I am just lucky my girlfriend was willing to have me back. I know I'm young but family is the most important thing in the world and I have responsibilities. You need someone to ground you. I'm quite happy at home with the kids, the curtains closed and doors shut.'

They had met at Woodside School, where she was in the year above Danny. He was smitten as soon as he met her but, for Joanne, he was 'just like my little best friend'. However, their friendship did eventually turn into something a bit more when, out of the blue, Joanne took the fourteen-year-old Danny down an alleyway and kissed him.

Danny recalled, 'We've known each other since we were twelve. She was the best-looking bird in the school – I was the ropiest boy. I was the naughty one – and she was the teacher's pet. She was an absolute raving sort and then suddenly asked if I'd go out with her. All the teachers hated it but girls like a bad boy.'

The relationship that followed would be a highly dramatic up-and-down one. As Danny has said in the past, they are 'either loved up to the eyeballs or hate each other with a passion'. Joanne has claimed that 'he means everything to me but there are days when he doesn't. He means nothing to me.'

In fact, if you're ever lucky enough to end up at their house, their fridge should let you know what mood they are in. Joanne stocks her fridge to reflect their relationship status. If they're loved up, you should expect to see a stocked-up fridge with plenty of food to choose from. But, if Danny has annoyed her once more, don't expect anything more than 'ham and butter' in there, according to Danny.

'We clash all the time,' he admits. 'She's an absolute straight-goer, never committed a crime in her life. We're chalk and cheese.'

Since they got back together, it seemed it would only be a matter of time before they would seal their relationship by getting married. Speaking in 2004, he revealed, 'Joanne is scared about this fame thing and where this film is going to take me. I am too. I like to think we'll get married but I want to be financially secure. I want to be sorted and choosing my roles. I don't want to be struggling and going up for *The Bill*.'

In another interview, he added, 'It's fucking hard. My girlfriend, who I've been with for fifteen years on and off, she's never been part of that game, so she finds it really hard at times. It's a hard game – either you're really rich and living it up or you're fucking skint and struggling – there's no in between. I'm also really shit with money when I've got it – I always spunk it, so I'm waiting for some real money so I don't need to worry about fuck all.'

However, despite being more financially secure than ever, in 2006 Joanne was still waiting. It was getting to the point that, whenever Danny put his hands in his pocket, she was waiting for a ring to come out. 'I want to keep her on her toes and I'm going to propose when she least expects it,' he teased.

They finally got engaged in 2008 after a sixteen-year on-and-off relationship, and it should come as no surprise to learn that it wasn't exactly rose petals strewn on the floor, ring in a glass of champagne, violinist in the background and a suited-up Danny on bended knee. Nope, it was, in fact, Joanne who proposed. It was done at 4am after a jovial, drunken night out. Knowing he would say yes in his drunken state, she admitted that she had taken advantage of him.

However, it should be stressed that Danny, far from his hardman image, is a caring and thoughtful fiancé, who regularly runs her a bath or massages her feet.

'Danny's romantic. Every now and then he'll do something and I'm like, "Awww,"' said Joanne.

But, in an interview with the *Observer* in 2007, he was quick to stress otherwise. 'They think they want the gentleman who's going to turn up with flowers and then do the ironing but actually it bores them to tears. I'm useless but she loves me for what I am. Women want so many different things. Some just want a pound note. Some want a Lear jet. Others want you to run them a nice bath, put the candles out, get them a nice bit of crispy duck, maybe a few spring rolls, get their nightie ready for when they get out of the bath and then brush their hair. Geezers just want to see a pair of tits. But in a romantic way, obviously!'

They have a tempestuous relationship, as seen on the 2008 panel show *Mr & Mrs*, when Joanne revealed that after one heated argument she attacked his Porsche with a broom. 'She was bang out of order. That really upset me,' he told the show's hosts Phillip Schofield and Fern Britton.

In fact, he was shocked that Joanne agreed to appear on the show. 'My missus has never wanted to do stuff like that, and then she says she wants to go on one of the cheesiest shows out there and talk about us as a couple to Fern and Phil.'

However, Danny revealed that their relationship is so volatile that they had an argument on the way to the studio! 'But she came across really well in the end,' he told Wharf.co.uk.

He told the *Daily Star* that on one occasion he ended up crashing into bed at 6am after a night out. Let's just say that Joanne was not amused. 'She took one look at me and told me I was a fucking idiot.'

Another recent setback saw Danny being put back in the doghouse, after his reported three-day bender didn't go down too well. However, Danny was determined to behave better, telling the *Mirror* shortly after at a Fila charity auction, 'I've got a lot of grovelling to do but hopefully things will get sorted.'

He is quick to admit that Joanna is his rock. 'Jo is the fucking love of my life. She keeps me in check,' he said to the *Daily Star*.

One thing that Joanne understandably struggles with is when Danny films a sex scene – most notably his steamy clinches with *X-Files* beauty Gillian Anderson in the 2007 vigilante drama *Straightheads*.

He said, 'It's an odd thing to do. I've got a girlfriend, got a daughter. It's really weird to have the licence to kiss somebody else and be naughty with somebody else. They are what they are really. They're not usually sexy things to do but it's a major part of the game. You've just got to get on with it. I know my old woman is not happy at the moment. She always gets the hump when I've got a sex scene. But she doesn't mind spending my dough so she's got to understand how I earn it.'

Despite their setbacks, Danny remains convinced she is the one he is going to spend the rest of his life with. 'I'm going to marry Joanne one day. She wants flamingos and little midgets running around with trays of food. But I don't mind going down the registry office, then for a few prawn vol-au-vents at the working men's club, home by half twelve. It's the woman's day though. It's about her being a princess.'

He remarked to *The Sun*, 'I do want to get married to Joanne. But it does frighten me, this marriage game. I've been to a few weddings recently and I'm not religious, I'd never been before in my life. All this traditional getting married in a church, with everyone standing there embarrassed about singing a hymn and it's all so serious. I don't like that. I wanna have a laugh when I get married. I want people to clap and cheer when we have that kiss at the end. I want people to have pie and mash for dinner. I want my own little take on it. All I'm going to be doing is worrying if there's enough vol-au-vents about and if my mum is getting on with her mum. But of course I wanna marry her. It has to be done eventually.'

Chapter Eleven

Danny's World Cup Adventure

He got stuck in and mucked in. I'll always
respect him for that – Richard Nockles,
co-director of *The Other Half*

While his role in *The Football Factory* propelled him back into the spotlight, Danny hadn't quite finished with football. However, *The Other Half* was as far removed from the plot of *The Football Factory* as it possibly could be. When you consider how much fuss was made with the media's absurd assumption that the film would cause normal football fans to give their common sense a good kicking, down 100 Stellas and head to Euro 2004 in a blaze of lager-fuelled animosity with only destruction in mind, it's ironic that Danny's next film showed a far less violent side of an English football fan.

Not that his character didn't have his own issues. 'Mark is a nice lad and is not a hooligan,' explained Danny. 'He thinks he can have a honeymoon and still go to the football, even though he hasn't told his wife.'

And that is essentially the main plot. The film represented a chance for the first, and so far last, time for

Danny to star as a romantic leading man. The low-budget movie (it was made for £150,000) sees Danny play Mark, a typical football man who takes his American bride, Holly (played by *Shameless* star Gillian Kearney), to Portugal – with the duplicitous idea of sneaking to the England games – during Euro 2004.

'I got to go and see all the England games. We used the final matches in the film so I was hoping they would go all the way but, of course, it wasn't the case,' Danny said.

Tiffany Whittome recalls the film's origin. 'I met with an old director friend who had co-written half a dozen drafts of *The Other Half* in February 2004. I loved the script and decided to do it, even though it involved filming at the Euros, starting in Portugal in just a few months' time. The money was raised quickly, privately, partly because we got Vinnie Jones attached early on.'

And the film reunited Danny with his *Mean Machine* co-star Vinnie Jones. Danny had said in the past that he felt excluded of sorts from the Guy Ritchie clique, so it must have been some source of amusement to learn that Vinnie would, in fact, be the supporting actor to Danny's leading man. However, despite the fluffy premise, it was to be an eventful shoot.

The film came to fruition from Richard Nockles, who co-wrote and co-directed the film alongside Marlowe Fawcett. 'When we came up with this idea it was a really low-key idea. We thought we would get actors fresh out of college and shoot it documentary style. But as we were writing the script we just became cocky bastards and we just thought, Fuck it, and we sent out the script to everyone to see what would happen. And we sent it to De Niro, everyone. But because we had no fucking money it was obvious that we would have to stick to British actors. A friend of mine saw Danny in a play in New York and he was like, "He's brilliant, you've got to get him involved."'

Danny was asked to audition and, fortuitously, it was Kearney who he was paired with. As soon as Nockles saw their audition, he knew that they were the ones that he wanted. 'The two of them were brilliant, the chemistry was amazing. I felt sorry for the other actors who turned up because no one else came close,' said Nockles. He insists there was no doubt Danny could handle a dip into previously uncharted territories – romantic leading man. 'Danny is an exceptional actor. He could do anything if he wanted. We weren't worried whatsoever. He was essentially playing a lad's lad but, for the character's sensitive side, he nailed it in the casting. There was not a shadow of doubt in my mind that he wouldn't be a success.'

It was then just the tricky business of managing to persuade Danny that this was a low-budget feature and that he shouldn't expect much of a payday. However, Nockles didn't count on the lure of the Euros for the football-loving actor. As soon as Danny found out he could go to England's qualifying games his, 'eyes lit up like a little kid saying yes', said Nockles with a laugh. 'But pretty much everyone was there for the football. There might have been a couple who thought we were making a film but it was really just an excuse to get us to Portugal!'

They began filming on 9 June 2004 in Lisbon, which was now crammed with thousands of football fans. Whittome explained in an interview with britishfilmmagazine.com, 'Due to the Euros, accommodation was sparse and expensive so the crew lived in a yoga retreat outside of Lisbon. But there were benefits – the police were sometimes flexible about permits to film and the backdrops for our locations were amazing... English flags and fans were everywhere and the streets were stunningly decorated for the festival of Saint Antonio.'

First-time director Richard Nockles admits that he hadn't quite thought through what he was embarking on for his movie debut. 'Shoot it in your living room over a series of weeks. That's the way you make your first film. Keep it small, keep it simple. I, however, decided to move twenty people across the world to the one location we've never been before – into the biggest football tournament in the world, with loads of security issues, and expected to just get away with it.'

Straight away Danny knew this wasn't any normal film shoot and was shocked at how unprepared everyone was. He says on the film's documentary, 'We arrive in Portugal and, basically, there's no call sheets or nothing like that. We just get up and I go, "OK, what's happening today?" And they say, "Right, what we're going to do is go to this location and nick some shots." I'm like, "I'm with you. No call sheets, no structure, nothing really planned. Fair enough, let's go for it."'

And Nockles was delighted at Danny's attitude because it represented the only way the shoot could work. Shortly before the shoot, he said, 'The actors we have, George Calil and Danny Dyer – the two male actors are both, I have a feeling, lunatics. But I honestly don't think anyone's sane. It's so funny. So there is just this collection of mad men going to Portugal. I have a feeling that maybe this is the only way we can pull it off because it's pure madness.'

Certainly, shooting it in the midst of a major football tournament with no idea what the final result was going to be was always going to represent some sort of drama.

Also, there was the little problem of what to do with regard to the football support. With the FA's fears that English football hooligans could dominate the front as well as the back pages of the newspapers, the filmmakers were obviously wary of letting Danny and Gillian walk into a real crowd of football fans. Without any script, or planning permission, Danny felt there was a danger it could all kick off.

'The main problem for us was the England fans,' said Danny. 'Well, what we thought anyway because we didn't know how it was going to play out. And the England fans have obviously got a reputation. And before any major tournament there is a big thing in the press about, if England fans play up, they're going to get thrown out of the tournament. So we're going out and filming in the middle of that and we don't know whether it's going to kick off. We don't have any permits to go anywhere but we want to catch it so it's raw, catch stuff that's real. Are we going to get battered and get all our stuff taken from us? What's going to happen here? We shouldn't be there, we have no permit so we haven't got a leg to stand on.'

Nockles continue, 'When we took Danny and Gillian

into thousands and thousands of England fans, you could see by their faces that they were like "Is this for real?" I got my mate Stu to be a security guard for them. By the way, Stu has never done any security before and, basically, the last line of defence for Danny and Gillian against these big, fuck-off people was my skinny mate Stu. It was crazy. Luckily, Danny has that wonderful ability to puff himself up bigger than he actually is. But for fucks sake, if anything had gone wrong, if anyone had taken offence, Jesus! *The Football Factory* had just come three months before and he was being recognised by these big English monsters and manhandled by them.' Affectionately it turns out.

Walking slowly towards the Rossio Square, which had now been taken over by exuberant England fans and was awash with flags, scarves, lager in the air and high spirits, they ended up filming the scene no problem. 'I think it's amazing we pulled that off really,' recalled Danny. In fact, despite having no permits at all and forced to snatch shots whenever they could, they only got hassle from the police once.

One of the main advantages of the film for Danny was the chance to see England play at the Euros – and it was a chance that the football fan jumped at. He had never been to a major tournament before so this was a huge thing for Danny.

'He was fucking brilliant,' remembered Nockles. 'He was there to do a job and watch football. We'd meet up after at the bar, have a drink and watch the games, and play football between shots. There was always someone with a football so we had lots of games.'

On 13 June 2004, England played France at the Estadio da Luz, Lisbon, and Danny was overjoyed to be there. Again it was filmed guerrilla style with Richard shooting from a block of flats overlooking the stadium. The plan was to shoot Danny entering the stadium, again without a permit. As Danny was walking up to the stadium not knowing whether they were getting the shot or not, he was suddenly worried because, as soon as he handed the ticket to the security guard, there was no way he would be allowed back out. Not that there was any danger of Danny leaving the game. He was in the stadium and had no intention of going anywhere.

That seemed a very good choice, as England ended up being in front through a Frank Lampard goal and, when he wheeled off in celebration, he ended up running right to the corner where Danny was sitting.

Unfortunately, it wasn't to last and France scored two quick goals in succession towards the end. 'It was absolute devastating,' revealed Danny.

There was more drama to come on and off the pitch. The next scene saw Danny and Gillian in a driving scene. Again, because they had no money and they could just afford one car, the onus was on Gillian not to crash.

Danny remembered, 'I just remember she was driving along and, oh, God, just missing cars by that much [he holds arms not far apart]. I was like, oh, God, I've got to concentrate on my dialogue while she's holding my gaze for too long. We were just missing traffic. Obviously everyone is panicking about the car but you actually had two actors in that car shitting their pants. Well, I don't know about Gillian.'

Lo and behold, the car ended up crashing into a ditch, with the bonnet being damaged. They then had to shoot the car from different angles.

The next game was against Switzerland and it's one that England had to win or they would be out of the tournament. For the filmmakers, too, if England went out at this stage, the film was pretty much over. Although, with Danny being Danny, there was only one of those scenarios that he was concerned about.

In the 'making of' he revealed, 'There is everything riding on this game because, not only are we out of the tournament if we lose, but it's the end of the film. There is no way we can go with the film really but I was so focused on the game I was thinking, Fuck the film. Richard and Tiffany are worried about the film, obviously, because that's why we are here. Every second of the day costs money. But I couldn't give a fuck about that at that stage. That sounds really bad but all I was worried about was England winning.'

Luckily for Danny, England did win (3–0 thanks to a Wayne Rooney double and a Gerrard goal late on) and they ended up winning the next game against Croatia to book themselves a quarter-final place against the tournament hosts, Portugal.

And so the film could keep on shooting, although some tension was brewing in the camp. 'It was a stressful shoot,' admitted Nockles. 'The only time I ever had the slightest bit of trouble with Danny was on a very hot, hot day and

I had him walk three miles across sand dunes just to get this one shot, which we never ended up doing. So he lost his rag a bit and huffed and puffed, and that was it. And to be perfectly honest he was quite within his rights to do so. Interestingly, he can get impatient at times. He's so good at acting that he usually nails his takes first time. Gillian, however, would take longer to warm up. Then he would start to get a bit pissed off. But Gillian would be at her best by the fourth take so there would be this weird balance between them.'

To keep Danny sweet, he was given the only ticket to the Croatia game – something that made him very happy indeed.

One of the scenes in the film proved less happy for him, however. The scene features a drunken Danny returning to the hotel and, in a bid to seduce his new bride, he undresses seductively, but soon falls asleep. But it wasn't the undressing scene that caused him to be red faced, more the fact that his drunken behaviour made him realise that this is actually what he is like when drunk!

One of the main problems was that the film's meagre budget meant lots of commuting – and the on-set catering left a lot to be desired. According to some of the crew, they were fed Alpen bars and, when they complained, they just changed the variety of the bars!

'It's quite an important thing, catering,' said Danny. 'You need to eat because it gives you energy. But if you don't know if you're going to have lunch that day, obviously that's going to cause a little bit of stress among the camp.'

'For Danny and Gillian, it wasn't as bad… as [for] the crew,' said Nockles. 'We couldn't take the piss with them because we might as well have shot ourselves in the foot. We couldn't feed our crew in five-star restaurants when you have no money so we had to do what we could do. I mean, I'm sure Danny and Gillian had their fair share of Alpen bars as well but we made sure Danny had a big, fuck-off steak at the end of the day.'

It should be stated that the catering improved considerably with no Alpen bars in sight when movie hardman Vinnie Jones came to film his short scenes as Danny's imaginary life coach!

And no doubt Danny must have felt a bit nervous meeting up with his *Mean Machine* co-star – an experience that he didn't look on with exactly fond memories. Danny hadn't been shy of having a few verbal digs at Vinnie. 'I ain't got no respect for him as a fucking actor. He ain't worth the steam off my piss at the end of the day,' he had remarked in the past.

'Let's just say they didn't exactly greet each other like long-lost brothers,' explained Nockles.

Danny, however, wasn't so diplomatic when speaking on his official website. 'One cunt who has pissed me off is Vinnie bloody Jones, who I thought was all right [when I] did *Mean Machine* with him. He is what he fucking is. But when I did *The Other Half* we did his scenes and his dialogue, but, when the camera turned around on me to do my bit, he fucked off to watch the golf. You don't do things like that. So this poor girl, the runner, had to read his lines for me. But, to be straight with you, the girl reading was better than fucking him. Speaks for its fucking self.'

'But that's the thing that freaks me out about actors in general,' added Nockles. 'You know, they're just so good at what they do. You ask them to turn it on, they turn it on. Danny's incredible. That scene I was telling you about when he was f'ing and blinding at me – that was actually the final scene of the movie, where he has the passionate-kiss scene… So he'll be swearing at me and then a minute after he will be passionately kissing his co-actor!'

But on-set tension aside, it was on to the quarter-finals. If England were to lose, it wouldn't have mattered much to the film. Again, that was the furthest thing from Danny's mind. 'By that stage, we had shot quite a lot of the film and, scriptwise, it didn't really matter if we went out at that stage. But fuck all that bollocks, I wanted England to win. It was a major game for us. If we had beaten them, we'd have well gone on to win that tournament because look who won that – Greece. I mean, come on. We lost on penalties. It was a really bad fucking moment. I remember the Portuguese being so happy – they're nice people but that night I despised them.'

That night, however, Danny decided to let himself loose on the Portuguese nightlife with Nockles, something the director remembered fondly. 'We got fucking smashed and he kept saying to me in his cockney accent, "Fucking hell, we should have done this right at the beginning, mate. You're all right. You're all right."'

Danny looked back on the film with fond, if bemused, memories. It showed that the boy from working-class stock wasn't afraid to get stuck in when things were tough. 'We did it. We went to Portugal with no money, no crew and we just got our hands dirty and we did it, man. 'Tis a beautiful thing.'

Nockles can't speak highly enough of Danny and there is one story in particular that he cherishes. 'This just shows you how fucking cool Danny Dyer is. Because we didn't have money and it was all last-minute planned, we only tried to book accommodation with three weeks to go. Now, any fucking moron would tell you that the chance of getting accommodation at the European finals three weeks before would be zilch. There were no hotels in the whole of Lisbon or surrounding area. We found a production company in Portugal who booted their grandmother out of their flat to give way for Gillian and Danny. Gillian got the grandmother's room. Danny was in this tiny room that was pretty much a nursery room. The only thing we could put in there was a blow-up mattress. Jesus Christ, he would have been perfectly justified walking out – a blow-up mattress in Granny's nursery room – it was like Harry Potter. The big plan was that after a week we could stay in this yoga retreat a mile away from Lisbon. We came down and it was your classic new-age hippy commune. Danny took one look and said, "No chance." He preferred to stay on the blow-up bed for seven weeks! I will always love Danny Dyer. He could have so easily been a dick about it like so many others would and he didn't. He got stuck in and mucked in. I'll always respect him for that.'

However, despite all the cast and crew's best efforts, the

film wasn't very well received. The main gripe was that, for a football film, there is no actual football in it. This was purely because they couldn't afford the footage, despite begging the FA and Fifa that they were making 'a nice little football film'.

'Lots of people got upset about it because they expected to see one thing but it's a completely different thing. I'm incredibly proud of it because what we all achieved for that budget was unbelievable,' said Nockles. 'If we could have had more money, it would have been better.'

Despite its flaws, Danny is a charismatic, romantic leading man and should really attempt to do another one. It surprised Nockles, who said, 'Danny definitely has that Hollywood look about him.'

At the end of the shoot, despite all the setbacks, the hitches and the occasional tantrums, Danny only had one regret. 'How weird was it to think England were going to win the tournament and we would be there for the whole ride? We were going to catch it all on film and it's going to be beautiful and it's going to have a big romantic ending with me and my wife in the middle of the England fans. They have an argument but then they both watch the final and England win the game. What a lot of bollocks that turned out to be!'

Chapter Twelve

Controversy in Cannes

That's a dirty film, that is

Forget the drug, hooliganism and vigilante-condoning claims from the media on films such as *Human Traffic*, *The Football Factory* and *Outlaw* – nothing caused the same amount of controversy for a Danny Dyer film quite like Thomas Clay's *The Great Ecstasy of Robert Carmichael*.

Scores of people walked out during the Cannes screening in disgust, with one film reviewer calling it 'so violent it makes [Stanley] Kubrick's *Clockwork Orange* look like a Britney Spears video'.

It was made during Danny's lean period and, although he loves controversy, it's doubtful that, had he known quite how much fuss would be made about the film, he would have chosen to do it. He has claimed since the media furore that it was less a passion project, more a need to pick up a pay cheque.

Thomas Clay had previously made *Motion*, a 2001 dour,

almost silent drama focusing on a homeless man in an English costal town. However, if Clay expected to be hailed as the new Ken Loach, he would be sorely mistaken. *Variety* described the short film as having 'precious little poetry and an immature grasp of the medium'.

The young filmmaker was undeterred, however. He set about making his full-length debut effort, hoping to make a huge impact and establish his name as one to watch. And his tale of a group of disillusioned youngsters in the seaside resort of Newhaven, and one scene in particular, would certainly make an impact. The film follows the life of Robert Carmichael, a bright student, but the product of a restless and violent environment in a small English costal town, set against the backdrop of the invasion of Iraq – which is seen constantly through news channels on TV. Carmichael and his two other friends amble through life without moral boundaries, the result of which ends up with their committing a horrific and visually traumatic crime – the gruesome torture and murder of a TV chef at his home and the brutal rape of his wife.

Danny and British actress Lesley Manville (who plays Carmichael's mum), as alongside famous cinematographer Giorgos Arvanitis, were the only familiar people on the set, with the rest of the cast all amateurs.

Revealing why he chose Danny for the part of Larry Haydn – a convict who kickstarts the terrible events that follow – Clay said, 'I wanted to cast people who had some relationship to the characters. Obviously, none of the actors are so disturbed in the way the characters are but they still have an affinity with the way they speak, understanding all the terminology of the drug world.'

Danny appears half an hour in, with his character celebrating his release from prison after eighteen months inside. 'In the clink, mate, for possession and aggravated assault,' he says.

He befriends his cousin John Kramer's gang and the unshaven, baseball-cap-wearing Larry is soon flirting with two giggling schoolgirls. Carmichael is instantly taken in by Larry's charms. However, things take a dark turn when Danny's character is at a house party and takes a girl into the room, then precedes to start off a mass gang rape. Although it is unseen by the viewers, it's an obviously disturbing scene. However, something far more horrific is to come.

Danny, however, had no idea how controversial the film was going to be, as he had only read his lines in the script and his character plays no part in the film's most shocking moment. He said, 'I just read for my bit. It's a character I've done a million times before but I quite liked the dialogue in it. There was something quite different about it.' But Danny was to get a shock when he read the whole script. 'It was this really mad fucking script,' he is quoted in the film's production notes. 'It's way out there. I like doing weird things, things that aren't the run-of-the-mill bollocks. Things that will be a bit controversial.'

It was a case of being careful what you wish for. When it premiered at Cannes, it was met with a stunned reaction. The rape scene was deemed 'excruciating beyond any in memory' and 'flirted with video-nasty territory' as the wife is raped repeatedly by the gang before she is assaulted with a bottle and left to bleed to death.

The BBC noted, 'It builds towards a stomach-churning home-invasion sequence sure to distress and/or enrage. Shot with dazzling brilliance, it's a bleak anti-seaside postcard of the state we're in: you'll wish you weren't here.'

'Veteran cinematographer Giorgos Arvanitis makes Newhaven look truly like the last place on God's list. But it's a shame that such obvious talent has gone into a film that seems to think "bleak and nasty" equates to "cutting edge and uncompromising",' said another review.

However, the *Daily Mirror* gave it its most damning critique. Giving the film no stars out of five, it ranted, 'There has never been a movie like this before. Pray to God there's never a movie like it ever again. With news reports of the invasion of Iraq popping up here and there, director Thomas Clay attempts to use the horrors of war as a fig leaf of respectability. Crap. Anyone who churns out perverted rubbish like this needs to see a shrink – and fast. Some of my fellow critics on the "serious" papers will, no doubt, refer to the film as provocative, important and challenging. Don't believe a word of it. Avoid this odious movie at all costs.'

Writer/producer Joseph Lang defended the film and, in particular, the second rape scene, saying, 'Yes, it is a very violent film, but it's a film about the alienation of youth. The rape is there to make you think. This is what happens in the name of the state, because of our governments, regularly in countries around the world. People need reminding that this is what violence is actually like. It should revolt and disgust you when people do certain things. In Tarantino films, we laugh when a man gets raped by another man. In ours, someone gets raped and you can't help but feel shocked and appalled. Isn't that a good thing? I am not asking every film to be like this. But as long as its intentions are thoughtful and honest, I think it's OK. People close their eyes and turn away from the violence that is happening in the world. The people that walked out and the people who have been having these angry reactions just don't want to think about these things. But we should face up to it. Drama is a way you can try to get people to do that.'

And there were some positive reviews, with some French critics praising it for its gritty brutal realism. *Screen International Magazine* called it a 'disturbing state-of-the-nation wake-up call', with some critics drawing parallels with Michael Hanke's *Funny Games* and Stanley Kubrick's *A Clockwork Orange* – particularly the latter as *The Great Ecstasy of Robert Carmichael*'s rape scene is accompanied by a classical song.

The *Observer* said it was a 'schematic movie suggesting a serious but simplistic connection between government-sponsored violence and the violent work the devil finds for idle hands'.

The *Independent* remarked, 'It's a horrible film to sit through, but that may not stop you looking out for Clay's name in future.'

Variety's review, in particular, was fulsome in its praise of the film's cinematography ('breathtaking') but claiming the film 'plays like the work of an extremely talented but still jeune filmmaker, who on a more practical level has a long way to go yet in terms of working with thesps. Some of the strident, stiff performances here rival those in Brit-kid show *Grange Hill* for drama-school clunkiness'.

A bemused Clay told EuropeanFilms.net about the reason for the violent content. 'What I believe can make people uncomfortable in *Carmichael* is the implication of the violence – to accept that Robert, a previously sympathetic character and a young man that we might see walking down our own street, would commit this act forces the viewer to address all sorts of uncomfortable questions. Yet this is precisely why it is essential to end the film in that way. It would seem my world view and the outlook of my film is controversial. However, many people have been extremely supportive and I'm very grateful for that. At the opposite end of the spectrum, the film must be having an impact to make people quite so vitriolic, whether they care to admit it or not.'

Daniel Spencer was cast as the title character after being spotted at a local acting class in Newhaven. He was originally asked to play a much smaller part, however. Writing on the film's IMDB blog after some scathing comments, he wrote, 'The main roles for the film were cast in London [including the three boys]. I didn't know anything about the project, until the makers came to the town, that the film was being made to search for local extras. Newhaven is where I was from and I had attended a local acting class for about six years when Donna

Shilling [Alice in the movie] came to watch a class to pick extras for the media lesson at the fort scene. I was originally cast as Gary, the guy who is lining up for the first shot at the fort, who has one line: "OK, I think." I was chuffed. But then a couple of days later Donna had obviously spread the good word about me and I got a phone call to say that they wanted me to audition for the main part because they were not happy with the actor they originally chose.'

Despite being involved in the graphic scene, Daniel was shocked by the controversy. He claimed, 'I was not aware that the last scene would cause so much controversy. I knew that it was a shocking and disturbing scene but what I didn't expect was that it could actually make people angry or upset.'

And the young actor certainly got a shock at the Cannes reception. 'It was a real eye opener for me when women were walking out crying, etc. I had no real problem with the scene and I knew I had to be professional about it but, as my first acting role, it was a baptism of fire.'

However, in interviews following the controversy, Danny seemed to do his best to distance himself from the film. He told the *Mirror* in 2005, 'I'm in no position to pick and choose my roles; I'm still a jobbing actor with a nine-year-old daughter who needs to be fed. I thought the script was really heavy but I had no money, so I did it. I didn't hear anything about it again until someone told me people were walking out of the screenings.'

And in *Attitude* magazine he explained further, 'That's

a dirty film, that is. I watched it at Cannes, with people being sick. The film is about a group of kids that get into rape, and they like it. It made me feel real fucking ill when I came out from seeing it. What audience wants to see a bird getting fucking raped though? I don't regret doing it because I thought it was going to be a film that would never see the light of day.'

Another thing that Danny struggled with was being one of the oldest cast members. 'It's a weird feeling. I don't know if I like it or not. But that's probably to do with getting older.'

While it attracted a huge amount of controversy, the film didn't prove to be the stepping stone the young cast of newcomers had hoped for. Daniel lamented, 'When all the hype has died down, what do I do? I wasn't in a financial situation to afford some time to look for an agent or roles, and I suppose I just sat back and waited for propositions. I am open to offers but what I don't want to do is become a wannabe actor begging for jobs – if you're not good enough, you're not good enough.'

Clay, meanwhile, went on to write and direct 2008 immigration drama *Soi Cowboy*. It earned far more positive reviews than his debut effort, with *Variety* saying it showed Clay demonstrating 'a growing maturity'.

Chapter Thirteen

The Holiday of a Lifetime

Riding about in a Porsche and running about with machine guns. It's every boy's dream, to be honest

If Danny thought he had got the role of a lifetime as Tommy Johnson in *The Football Factory*, he got just as strong a role in 2005's *The Business*. Written and directed again by Nick Love, it also featured a blistering intro monologue with Danny slipping into Love's dialogue with ease.

'My old man wrote me a letter from prison once. He said, if you don't want to end up like me, stay away from crime, women and drugs. Problem is, it doesn't leave you much else to do, does it?'

Right away, fans of *The Football Factory* could ease into the film like they could a pair of comfort slippers. However, Danny was wary that the voiceover could mean that audiences would find it too similar to his previous hit. He told cinema.com, 'It's important not to come across like Tommy Johnson, especially with the voiceover because I have got quite a distinctive voice. I didn't want to sound like him in any way. So my voiceover breaks up in the beginning and it sort of changes towards the end. I get greedy because it's all set in the 1980s and stuff, when cocaine started to come into England. It was the gangsters out in Spain who started it. They were earning lots of money and just getting greedy with it, and then it all falls down. That's when the voiceover changes again to, "What the fuck am I doing now? I'm stuck in this rut; I've got to get out of it."'

Set in the 1980s in Spain's 'Costa del Crime', the film revolves around Frankie, a London council-estate boy who flees to Spain to deliver a package to a man named The Playboy after he viciously beats up his mother's abusive boyfriend with a cricket bat.

The film's intent couldn't be more obvious – it's *GoodFellas* in flip flops; Scorsese and Sangria – a sun-drenched setting with a soundtrack that would fuel many a cheesy retro nightclub, including the likes of Duran Duran, Frankie Goes To Hollywood, Blondie and The Buggles.

The Playboy – in what is a towering performance by Tamer Hassan – immediately takes a liking to Frankie, who shows him the upside of the life that he has managed to make for himself after fleeing the country with his bank-robbery gang, The Peckham Four, after an armed robbery goes wrong.

Flash cars, swanky yachts, the best of the best from fashion that time forgot, and all the women and drink you could want at The Playboy's neon-soaked bar. As Frankie notes about his mentor, 'Everything he touched turned to gold – even his bed made itself in the morning.'

Even the introduction of Charlie's vicious business partner Sammy (Geoff Bell), who takes an immediate dislike to Frankie, is nothing more than a minor irritation. Frankie is finally living the life he has always dreamed of – he gets to be someone.

Unsurprisingly, the good times can't last for ever. Once the money piles up through the vast amount of drug dealing, so does the paranoia, double crossing and treachery. It's not long before the bright, sun-drenched visuals and sweeping vistas are being replaced by saturated dark and gritty close-ups.

The film's final third sees Frankie at his lowest ebb – with him and The Playboy covered in sweat and limping around like a pack of dogs, robbing houses for any scraps of drugs to sell on.

When The Playboy's attempt at a huge reunion party ends in an embarrassingly low turnout, Frankie decides on one last attempt at getting even with Sammy and his treacherous girlfriend Carly (played with fine femme-fatale charm by Georgina Chapman). Sammy finally gets his comeuppance when he is shot by police while Danny escapes through a sewage pipe covered in faeces (a special effect which was achieved by two kids in the pipe pumping out chocolate milkshake mixed with Rice Krispies!) and then, after dealing with Carly, he rides off into the sunset.

When the title credits reveal what has happened to each character, his one reads, rather cutely, 'Frankie went to Hollywood'.

However, Love's original idea for the film was somewhat

different to the one that he shot. He told FilmFocus, 'I actually wrote a treatment for this in 1995. When I conceived it, it was an ensemble piece. It was the drug business in Spain seen through three different eyes. So you saw it from the baron, the middleman and the street junkie. The problem was that they then made *Traffic*. It was a lot like that film but my idea was before it.'

He wrote the script after spending four weeks in Marbella after *The Football Factory* was released in the cinema. 'I was fascinated by the migration of the British communities in the 1980s, especially from London, and criminals on the run who sought out sun, sand and sangria in the southern coast of Spain, leaving behind the dreariness of the English weather in the hope of a better life. I wanted to explore the relationship between the ex-pat community and the Spanish people whose towns and villages were taken over. I came up with the idea for *The Business* because I was interested in this reverse migration and its effects on the locals (some opportunistic, like the mayor) and the way criminals on the run from the British police were forming a new sub-culture. Although *The Business* is not based on real characters or events, it does draw from a wide range of knowledge and stories based on people who have lived and still live on the Costa del Sol.'

Because of a land-ownership dispute over Gibraltar between the Spanish and British government, many British criminals took advantage of the minimal risk of being prosecuted or extradited in the Costa del Sol, although a new extradition treaty between the two countries in the late 1980s has since put a stop to that loophole.

For Nick, the chance to revisit the 1980s was an appealing prospect – as it was an era he was something of an expert on. 'Nick's obsessed with the 1980s,' said Danny. 'It's a big part of his life. So he was always going to make a film about that. I didn't know how or what but I knew it would be genius, whatever he did.'

What Love wanted to do was show the cool side of the 1980s. He explained, 'I always felt the 1980s was a cool decade that had somehow become the subject of ridicule and jokes down to some of the excessive hairdos and shoulder pads – but apart from that I thought the 1980s was a great decade for fashion and cutting-edge style. Not to mention musically inventive. We somehow lost sight of the cool stuff. Suddenly people have started revisiting the 1980s as a "cool decade". Designers are reissuing limited-edition 1980s clothes and the music is being sampled on every dance track – thus, I wanted to make a very British story that didn't feel laborious or dated but celebrated the style and culture of this era.'

His producing partners (once again Vertigo Films' Allan Niblo and James Richardson) were sceptical about the idea because they thought it would be impossible to make a film set in the 1980s cool. 'I said, "I've got this mad idea. I want to do a 1980s film." And I could see them going, "Fuck," because everyone associates the 1980s with bad hair and big shoulders, not with people looking cool.'

One thing you can't accuse *The Business* of not being is cool. That is something Love achieved with devastating effect. The film is soaked with (at the start anyway) bright, sun-drenched exteriors and neon-coated interiors.

Love kickstarted a comeback of Fila, Kappa and Sergio Tacchini gear. Clothes were so important for Love that he was scouring eBay for the gear as soon as the film had the green light. He said, 'Sportswear was the biggest male fashion style of the 1980s so my wizard costume designer Andrew Cox and myself went to painstaking efforts to get the detail right. And also, what people were wearing in Spain was different to what they wore back home. I remember everyone wearing Fila tennis shorts and Diadora Borg Elites in Spain, as it was so hot you couldn't wear jeans or suits really.'

Cox recalled, 'With Nick as my guide and mentor, and eBay as my best friend, I set about gathering the now vintage clothing for the film. Nick's passion for the decade and subject was infectious and admirable, and my incentive for ensuring everything was just right. I started my research on my own doorstep, digging out all the old reference photos and record covers... from there I scoured vintage magazines, newspapers and 1980 films and TV programmes, and began to build a picture of the decade. The next step was to actually source the clothes, the major obstacle being the available funds. It would have been easy with a Hollywood-sized budget to go to the costume houses and order this that and the other, and have it shipped out to Spain, but on this occasion it was not an option.'

However, Nick was so passionate that he would be bidding on eBay without Cox's knowledge and several times they were inadvertently outbidding each other, costing them 'a few unnecessary pounds'. 'Bidding became an obsession both for Nick in Spain and myself in the UK

– often we were up in the middle of the night, determined to place that winning bid,' Cox revealed.

If it wasn't scouring eBay, it was scouring shops, looking for vintage clothes. A task that wasn't easy for Cox. Especially when he had to jump between Spain and England. He explains, 'Filming in southern Spain proved to be an added challenge as it is not renowned for its vintage markets and shops. So having filmed all week in Spain, I would fly home late every Friday... shop all weekend at Camden, Portobello, etc. and fly back with bags full of clothing for the week ahead... One mad weekend I flew from Malaga to Luton on Saturday morning... ran around Camden like a madman all afternoon, jumped in a cab to Gatwick and flew back that evening to film early Sunday morning... easyJet became easyBed for me!' He added, 'I did, however, discover a small English charity shop in Nerja, which was stocked with clothes from all the ex-pats living out there... Many of the clothes were pure 1980s leftovers. Even in Almunecar, the town where we were based, the weekly market and many of the shops there sold such classic clothing it could have also been straight out of the 1980s... A godsend at times.'

The soundtrack was just as important for Love. They managed to get access to EMI's back catalogue after cutting a deal, which including the use of such songs as 'Echo Beach', 'Heart of Glass' and 'Video Killed the Radio Star'. The song highlights Frankie's welcome to his new world. 'Welcome to the Pleasuredome' by Frankie Goes To Hollywood was the only song that they had to purchase outright.

'It is very difficult to strike a balance between getting it correct in the detail but at the same time not putting the audience off with too much overpowering costume and music.' He continued on the film's production notes, 'We considered the music for a long time – and my producer Allan Niblo did an amazing job at clearing the songs in the film – some of the music in the film everyone will remember and other tracks will only jog certain memories. Most of the tunes will take the over-twenty-five audience back to a time and place. For me, the biggest track is Frankie Goes To Hollywood's "Welcome To The Pleasuredome" – this song defines the era, place and atmosphere like no other song. Everyone still remembers them as one of the best groups ever. Classic.'

However, while Love strived for authenticity, there were certain prop items that were too authentic. During the shoot, their props van was broken into but the thieves were no doubt stunned when they opened one of the boxes. In it was a large Louis Vuitton holdall stuffed with cash, ten kilos of Marijuana and cocaine, gun holders, ropes and binoculars.

While they were all fake props, the thieves didn't know that and, thinking they had just ripped off a local drug cartel, they dumped their stash on the roadside, seemingly fearing there would be deadly reprisals. The items were promptly picked by up the no doubt bemused local police. The poor production designer, Paul Burns, spent hours in the police station persuading police that they were fake and that they were for a film! It was only when the police tested the 'drugs' to determine if they were real or not that Burns was allowed to take them back.

Prop setbacks aside, Vertigo Films knew they were on to a winner again with Love. 'After reading the script, I spoke to James immediately, knowing that we had an exciting new film on our hands. The pace, veracity and emotional depth of the story was all that we expected and much, much more from Nick,' said Niblo.

Producer James Richardson added, 'Having a trusted team behind us made things so much easier for us and meant we could move quickly into pre-production. The casting was, again, very easy as Nick wrote the story with key actors in mind. He envisaged Danny Dyer playing Frankie, Charlie was written for Tamer Hassan, who had impressed Nick in *The Football Factory* as Millwall Jack, and the part of Sonny suited Roland Manookian to the ground.'

Once again Danny had no idea if he was gong to be in Love's next film. All he knew was that Love was working on it in Spain, and the first time he knew about the film was when the script was thrown on to his lap by the director and he was asked if he wanted to be the lead.

He told *Empire*, 'He went away for two months to Spain, sat on his own, didn't speak to anybody and came back with this. I read it and from there I knew exactly what I was going to do with it. And he didn't question me once – he lets me get on with it.'

After *The Football Factory* and *The Other Half*, Danny was now becoming used to being a leading man. Speaking to the *Mirror* in 2005, he said, 'I'm really chuffed. I've been acting for fifteen years and everything I've learned I put into that film. A lot of people come straight out of drama school and just don't know how to do it. Every actor wants a leading role but some aren't good enough.'

And the role of Frankie was one he was desperate to tackle. Which male wouldn't? 'Riding about in a Porsche and running about with machine guns. It's every boy's dream, to be honest. This is a really sexy film; I think it's going to put British gangster films on the map. This goes at a level that people have not seen before.'

Not only was Danny the lead role but it was also a chance to be more than just a laddy actor. It would eventually pose problems on set. Speaking while in Spain working on the film, he said, 'The hardest thing for me is shaking it off at the end of the day because my nut's all over the place at the moment because I'm so involved in this job. I'm obsessed with it, which is great when you are filming but not when you go home. I'm being a bit weird around my mum because I don't know who the fuck I am at the moment. Which I've never known as an actor before because I've never been that involved in a part before – never had an opportunity to go that method. For the final third of the film I'm quite unapproachable. I zoned out filming it. It was the only way. I looked a right fucking state.'

Danny got so close to the character that each different wardrobe and hairstyle representing a change in Danny's character would see him morphing into that role almost instantly. He was regularly told by the film's make-up girls that his whole mannerism changed as soon as he put the clothes on.

'It's hard to snap out of that but, as I said, I was obsessed with it and I couldn't blag this film for one second. And, of course, you don't film it in order, so, on one particular day, in the morning I'd be vulnerable Frankie, then have a bit of lunch and, in the afternoon, I'm deadbeat Frankie. And it's like having two different heads, having to snap between them. A good challenge as an actor, that's what you want to be doing.' And it took Danny a couple of weeks to shake off the character when the cameras stopped rolling. But he conceded, 'I couldn't do the job as well as I wanted to if I didn't go through that.'

Danny wasn't the only one who was tied to his character. Tamer Hassan also latched on to his role, as, just as *The Football Factory*'s Tommy Johnson was a breakthrough role for Danny, The Playboy was a chance for Tamer to show he could do more than just play the hoodlum sidekick.

Tamer had the time of his life with The Playboy, although he hated the comedown the character has in the film. In fact, the scene when The Playboy begins to turn on Frankie was a hard one to film for both of the actors – since their relationship was now becoming one that was as close as Danny and Love's.

'That stuff wasn't nice to play,' Danny admitted to *Empire*. 'Tamer is a great friend of mine and he's lovely. But he had to turn into this character that hates me and is horrible to me. We hated filming that stuff – it was not nice. I went into a mad zone in that segment of the film too, which I'd never done before as an actor, and it freaked me out a little bit.'

In fact, Frankie ended up being the hardest character

that Danny has ever played. He's forced to spend most of the film reacting to the more flamboyant characters that grace the film, while at the same time, voiceover aside, only relying on his stage presence to stand out.

And, unlike Tommy or Moff, Frankie was his first real character that actually grew in the film to become someone completely different from at the start.

Geoff Bell (who starred with Danny in *Mean Machine*) also puts in a fine performance as The Playboy's vicious business partner Sammy.

Richardson said of Bell, 'The part of Sammy was a little difficult to cast but, when Geoff Bell came in to audition, Nick, Allan and I knew he was the right person for the part. Geoff combined the malevolence, cunning and brutal nature the character was about – he nailed the part.'

That was something that excited Danny the most – working with Bell again. 'I'm good friends with Geoff,' said Danny. 'I remember at the *Mean Machine* premiere thinking, Wow, he's good, Bellsy. I remember thinking, I really want to work with him. He's the one that stood out for me. He's a great actor, very powerful in this.'

Casting Carly was a tough one for Love, as it's arguably the first proper female character that he has ever written. Getting the right woman to play her meant lots of auditions with young British actresses. Not that Danny minded too much. 'It's important,' he recalled to *Empire* in 2005. 'So we sat and auditioned ten birds, which was a lovely day. Georgina was the first one in and set a standard for everyone else, and nobody else could really match her. She's beautiful but, at the same time, she could bring out this snide way about her and was happy just to put aside the beauty. She was nervous on set because she was surrounded by us lot and we're all pals, we all know each other, so she came in and was really good about it. She was very passionate about it and that was the key – she wanted to get it right.'

Niblo added, 'We had seen lots of actresses for the part of Carly and there was press speculation at the time about who this part would go to. When Georgina Chapman came in to audition for us, she immediately outshone everyone else we had seen and we offered her the part immediately.'

Shot over eight weeks in the hot summer of Almunecar, a small village in southern Spain, the harsh, arduous weather conditions were hardly ideal for filming. 'It was boiling hot and the flies were fucking unbearable,' said Love. 'The difficult parts of the shoot were far and few between but I would say the scenes shot on the boats were the hardest, as the boats never kept still, so it's a continuity nightmare. It was very crammed with the crew on board and half of them got seasick. The orange-grove scenes were hard as well, as the heat felt very stifling. Also, there were some sort of horse flies lurking around and each day we'd wrap and find we'd been bitten forty to fifty times!' The weather was also exasperating the typical on-set arguments. Love revealed, 'Everyone had a meltdown. Me and Tamer had an argument on the boat.'

The film's setting was certainly different to what they were normally used to. Danny said in a 2005 interview with the BBC, 'Where we were staying was very native Spanish, nobody spoke English, so they really didn't take that much notice of us. That was a shock. We were filming up in the mountains and were quite out of the way most of the time. It wasn't a holiday vibe. We were filming in the mountains, living in a small town. [With no one speaking English] it wasn't a jolly-up.'

'[Nick] is a friend but when it comes to work he makes it very clear what he wants,' added Danny in an interview with cinema.com. 'He doesn't like messing about, which is why it always runs so smoothly. There is no fucking about on his set.'

Due credit to Nick, his ambition, drive and belief in the project seems to rub off on the cast. When the main characters – Danny, Tamer and Geoff – did manage to get a few hours together, much of the time was spent going over the film in minute detail. 'You get obsessed with it and by the end of it you're knackered,' he said.

Not that they didn't have their moments of fun. In a move that put new meaning to a DVD extra, Danny is seen getting his manhood out in the 'making of', something which actually shocked Danny himself.

He told *Attitude* magazine, 'For seven weeks we had a camera with us all the time. And on this one day, Tamer was being interviewed. And he was using all these long words and I thought I could walk up behind him with my cock out, while he was trying to make all these profound points. So I did that and they kept it in. Out of seven weeks of shooting they kept it in. They didn't even censor my cock out.'

However, despite the lavish extravagance on show, the film's budget was far less than you might expect. But Love was very canny with the money to fool audiences into thinking they were telling a multimillion-pound epic tale. Cars were hired, boats were hired and painted, Charlie's Bar was actually an already established bar with some neon slapped on to establish the time, shooting was done in rooms that they were actually staying in and the same group of extras was used constantly.

While promoting *The Football Factory*, Danny made it clear that he couldn't wait to film *The Business*. 'I can't wait to start filming abroad,' he said. 'The Algarve, then Spain. The missus and my little girl are coming over to join me. Beats six weeks in the backstreets of Bermondsey any day.'

His daughter Dani also appears in the film briefly, towards the end of the film at the crime family's meal. Even his beloved Nana Polly made the visit to Spain – something that makes Love laugh at the memory. 'I remember when she came down to Spain. It was about a hundred and thirty degrees, crickets everywhere and we were in this little town in the middle of nowhere. First thing she said to me was, "I want a nice McDonalds and to get my tits out in the sun."'

The Business also represented a film that he could show his family (his kids aside) – there were no pill-popping antics or the gritty violence of hooliganism here. It was a searing, almost fun, crime flick and his family loved it.

Speaking on the film's commentary track, he revealed, '[My dad] loved this film. I knew he would. He got all choked up. "Perfect," he said.'

Niblo was understandably delighted with the final product. He could clearly see that Love had a particular understanding of what a normal twenty-something male wants to see for escapism. He beamed as he said, 'We are ecstatic with the end result of the film. We thought *The Business* would be a great film but it has far exceeded what we expected. The story is so rich and vibrant, a contemporary fantasy with an edge and funny undertones. Nick Love was unrelentingly positive to everyone and always very clear about what he wanted, while leaving the actors enough room to experiment. This has translated brilliantly on to the big screen for all to see.'

Love added, 'I love it. I'm so proud of it. I feel it's such a "me film". It's got so much of me in it. The look, the style, the music, the attitude – all of it – I feel like it comes straight from me. It feels like a combination of both *The Football Factory* and *Goodbye Charlie Bright*. A mature version of both films and, having spent my last two films learning my craft, I feel that *The Business* is made with such confidence. If I never make another film after this, I think I'll still feel that my trilogy is complete.'

While the film was alternately praised for its slick directing and entertaining tale and derided for being too much gloss and not enough drama, Love defended his decision to make a film for a specific audience. 'Audiences are changing. People don't want to sit down for two and a half hours. You couldn't make *Apocalypse Now* and *Godfather* now,' he said. 'They're masterpieces but we know our audience is young men and they want to be entertained quickly. So we know that and you can't be self-indulgent. You've got to be thinking, Who's going to be punting £15 for this DVD? You've got to be thinking about it. [It's] not for *Guardian* readers or *Independent* readers. They would never admit it even if they liked it. They fucking despise [my films]. Fuck them.'

However, *Variety* heaped praise on the film and credited Danny for a 'subtly slow-burning performance'.

Love fired a parting shot at the British critics, claiming that they hate it when the British make successful movies. He told *The Times*, 'I have always thought, What's the point of spending three or four years on it for it to die a death? And ultimately, it's fucking irresponsible. If you don't make commercially minded films, you're killing the British film industry.'

Chapter Fourteen

Back in Business

I don't mind a bit of gay attention. It's all sweet.
As long as they're nice to me

The Business's success proved not only that was *The Football Factory* not a fluke, but also that Danny was now a bona fide leading man with a sizable audience to boot. The old adage of 'men want to be him, women want to be with him' was one that could definitely be applied to Danny. He was the cheeky chap who you could have a pint with, but watch your wallet as he might be away it when you back's turned. Meanwhile, for women, he was the roguish bit of rough who probably wouldn't remember your name the next day. Of course, none of these was quite true but that's the power of the movies and Danny's star was getting brighter and brighter.

His audience was to get bigger and bigger as well, because it wasn't just *FHM* readers that were now devoted to Danny. It seems he was attracting a whole new fan base.

Gay lifestyle magazine *Attitude* wanted Danny for their cover shoot. But their hopes were surely slim ones. They had no chance of getting an actor so identified with a heterosexual laddy persona, or did they?

'*Attitude* wanted Danny to pose naked and he said he would do it only if he got £500 in an envelope,' said James Stafford, the shoot's photographer. So off Stafford went to Canning Town to pick Danny up for the shoot. Armed with a brief of 'getting him naked without showing his dick or his arse' and a bottle of wine (*Attitude* said, 'If he's a bit shy on the day, give him a glass of wine'), he set off with some reservations. 'It's for a gay magazine and, because he's seen as a no-nonsense kind of person, I kept thinking, How's he going to take it?' The shoot didn't exactly get off to the greatest of starts. 'We were meant to be there at 9.30am and we got there about 9.15am. We knocked on his door and there was just no answer. I kept thinking, This is getting us nowhere. Turns out he actually saw we were there early and thought, I'm not letting him in.'

While it was an inauspicious start, the shoot would prove to be an eventful one. Danny was hesitant at first but alcohol would play a part in one of his most iconic photo shoots – and not just a bottle of wine, as he quickly realised that he needed more Dutch courage than a glass of Pinot Grigio would give him.

'He sent his agent to get him a bottle of brandy from the local Spar. And yes, he got drunk.'

The many pictures as a result included Danny clutching the bottle of brandy half naked, clutching his genitals fully naked and several other saucy shots that would have shocked his male hetero fan base and, no doubt, pleased his female ones.

However, there were several shots that you did not see. 'Because he's a bit of an exhibitionist, he did take all his clothes off and swung his dick around like a helicopter,' recalled Stafford.

The next morning Danny's agent frantically phoned Stafford. 'She kept saying, "Please don't send those pictures to anybody as he was really drunk."

'I said, "They've already gone to *Attitude*." And so I begged *Attitude* not to use the dick pictures. But they did go around to everybody in the office on an email! He was absolutely lovely but also a whirling dervish, completely out of control, but nice with it. He's just a really naturally sexy straight guy. He's not like the normal gay models, where they are all trimmed and plucked and buff. I don't think he works out, he's a naturally sexy, good-looking man.'

Stafford did concede that Danny thought he was probably going to get stick from his friends about the shoot. 'He lives in Canning Town so I can't imagine him hanging around a lot of poofs there,' said the photographer, who has worked with *Attitude* for over ten years now.

Of course, it's not like his friends would ever admit to seeing the interview, Danny admitted. 'The result is that my pals couldn't pick it up because it's a gay magazine but they were dying to do it. They were at a newsagent but they were like, "Oh, no." They just can't do it. They're East Londoners. They cannot be picking up gay magazines.'

In an interview with *Metro*, he added, 'I got a lot of grief for it but I don't give a fuck. I'm not queer. I've got nothing against queers – they're sweet as a nut – but it was a bit of a mad statement to make, being a bit of a laddy actor, and because I was promoting a documentary about football hooligans at the time. I was happy with the pictures but I still get grief for it and I accept that.'

Apart from the images, it was still left to Danny's big mouth to cause the most fuss. 'It's sweet if you like a bit of cock. You know, I've had me moments. I've had me fucking moments,' he told the interviewer. When pressed further, he claimed, 'We'll leave it at that.'

He recalled to Charlotte Church, 'They got me pissed and I was like, "You want me to strip? You want to see me nuts?"'

It wasn't the first time Danny was interviewed in a gay magazine – that honour belonged to *AXM* Magazine in 2004. It was another cover shoot but this time Danny was fully clothed. While it was a last-minute shoot because the original shoot with another actor was deemed unusable, Danny didn't care and was delighted to be finding a new audience. He said, 'It's all right, sweet as. I don't mind a bit of gay attention. It's all sweet. As long as they're nice to me, I don't give a fuck. I'll have a little bit of a flirt-up, a little bit of banter. I'm quite chuffed I'm doing this interview – it's not something I ever thought about before. I'm there for it, I'm up for it.'

Although it has to be said, don't expect to see many near-naked Danny Dyer pictures in the future – in gay or straight magazines. Not because he's embarrassed by them. It's just that, as he readily admits, he is starting to see the effects of getting older.

He said, 'Listen, I've been clocking this chin lately. I don't know what to do about it. There's nothing I can do, you can't do anything about it. I could be in a prisoner-of-war camp and not eat anything for fucking weeks and I'd still have a double chin. There is nothing I can do about it. I've got a bit of a belly. I mean, what the fuck is that all about? I used to be a heartthrob; I'm losing my wig. I quite like that though as I'm starting to evolve into something else a little bit. I quite like the idea of getting fat, growing a pair of tits and going bald, sitting in a big mansion, eating cake with the kids running about.'

As Nick Love jokes on his commentary for *Outlaw*, 'He's got a great face for the wireless these days. He's good for a voiceover, good for a DVD commentary.'

To alienate his hardcore geezer fan base further, in a feature for the *Sun* in 2008 he dabbled in 'man make-up'. To the shock of his fans, he admitted, 'I don't see anything wrong with men wearing make-up. I look after my skin – my face is my tool so I have to. I always moisturise and I'm not against a touch of fake tan. I know a lot of tough guys who, when I meet them, it's not unusual for us to discuss which facials, moisturiser and eyebrow-plucking techniques we use! I've used liner and mascara for a film premiere. Anything that gives you an edge with pulling the birds is a bonus.'

However, surgery is not an option. He growled to the *Daily Star*, 'Does it look like I've had botox? It's better for guys than girls. We don't get older, we get distinguished. I fucking love getting older. I'm more sorted. I've got my bird and I'll have two kids this year. I'm not about to do something stupid like staying out drinking all night.'

It's testament to Danny's likeable persona that he can appeal to such a wide-ranging audience. 'To be on the front of a queer magazine with my top off and then go around the country talking to hooligans – I don't think there are many people who could get away with that,' he told *Metro* in 2007.

Danny is who he is. For his working-class male fans, Danny represents one of their own. And he was gong to cement his relationship with his laddish male fan base by his two new friends – a co-star and a lifelong idol.

Chapter Fifteen

Danny and Friends

Tamer's my pal. He's always been good to me.

The success of *The Business* suddenly saw Danny in lads mags and on chat shows everywhere. Brands wanted to be associated with him as he proved an 'inroad' to the working class who weren't buying into whatever the metrosexual man of choice (Jude Law, David Beckham, etc.) were selling. In their eyes, Danny was one of them.

As was his *The Football Factory* and *The Business* co-star Tamer Hassan. The pair were to be regularly seen in nightclubs, where they would be paid quite handsomely for their many personal appearances. No wonder, as the clubs would be packed full of punters desperate to see their two idols in the flesh.

The pair became pals almost instantly on *The Football Factory*. 'We just hit it off,' Hassan told the BBC. 'It's like a big brother, little brother thing. He's just one of those kids who you've got to look after and take him under your wing. He's such a lovely boy, you just [want] to do things for him and want him around all the time. Everyone loves him.'

The two would go on to become the faces of sportswear giants Fila thanks to their work on *The Business* and, in 2008, they would appear in a memorable viral film to promote Fila's Vintage White Line Collection.

Fila's UK marketing manager Marc Travis said, 'Danny and Tamer both starred in *The Business* in 2005 and the film was a Fila vintage-sportswear fest. The film sparked a cult following and there was a natural connection between the boys and the product so we got them involved officially as brand ambassadors. We've done some great stuff with them over the year and thought making a short film would really engage with our consumer and their fans.'

The ad saw Danny and Tamer play two South London gangsters who are given their next target, an Italian outfit who have the front to reappear after twenty years. 'I don't want you to scare them; I want you to make them sorry, really fucking sorry. I want the pair of them laced up by Friday,' they are told.

They get their targets and brutally torture them – only for the camera to pull back and reveal the Centre Court line – new trainers that have been aged to replicate a 1980s lived-in trainer. 'We break them in for you... Get the look without the effort' is the ad's strapline.

'We found a real gem in the form of director Marcus Jones; he grew up with the Fila brand in the 1980s and loves the gangster genre that we were wanting to recreate. So, in our first meeting to discuss Fila producing a gangster spoof starring Danny Dyer and Tamer Hassan, I just saw his eyes light up and his brain kick into gear with loads of creative ideas,' said Travis. 'The concept was pretty much sorted in that first meeting but what makes the film is the clever scriptwriting, which subtly references the brand's heritage and product throughout. The benefit of working with Danny and Tamer was we got the whole thing shot in one long day and then it was over to Marcus and his team for the edit. The concept arose from a creative brainstorm with our team – we wanted to make the most of having Danny and Tamer on board and we had some great new "trotters" with a stone-washed leather treatment. From there it sparked some ideas about how much fun you could have creating that authentic "worn-out" look. The benefit of working with two British actors that are known for their cult following and hard-hitting movies meant it all fell into place. What did we want to portray? That as a brand we are evolving and, hopefully, show that we are having a bit of fun along the way!'

For the fans it was a welcome chance to see the pair on screen again – even for a brief moment. And the fans want to see them together just as much as Hassan wants to. He said, 'For a moviemaker to get that dynamic on screen, it's a no brainer. This is the genius of Nick Love. He saw how we instantly fell in love and used that dynamic to write *The Business*. Apparently, there's a big British outcry for me and Danny to do another film together.

We're like that in life, we're so close. He's like my little brother. I adore the ground he walks on. We do PAs together, signings together, we drink together. We literally live in each other's pockets.'

Despite Hassan's considerable physical stature, he was the one who was nervous the first time they met each other. He recalls, 'I was a fan of Danny for years. I used to adore watching him on screen. I first met him in a pub and was mesmerised by him. He's probably one of the funniest kids you'll ever meet in your life and his dialogue is second to none. When I heard Danny might be cast for *Football Factory*, I was rooting for him, saying, "You've got to give him the job." I know it sounds wanky because people look at Danny Dyer and say, "He's not De Niro, what are you talking about?" For me, it wasn't him as an actor but him as a person. I couldn't get enough of him. From that day we got on.'

In 2007, the pair joined the likes of supermodel Caprice, rapper Xzibit and *Star Wars* actor Hayden Christensen at the Gumball 3000 Rally. The event sees celeb and playboy petrol heads driving across Europe, including Athens and Berlin, before finishing in London's Trafalgar Square just in time for a star-studded party.

And the £28,000 entry fee didn't deter Danny and Tamer from getting behind the wheel. But they didn't exactly have the best preparation, looking shattered after a heavy session celebrating the birth of Danny's second child Sunnie two days after she was born. 'Do you think I'm a wrong 'un for doing the Gumball Rally two days after my little one's been born?' he asked a female TV presenter from *Rare*.

But off the pair went in the gold Range Rover Sport. 'I am a big fan of cars and I did the Gumball Rally this year,' said Hassan. 'Me and Danny did a documentary about the rally and we had a film crew with us, filming us in a Range Rover Sport, which was sort of an upgrade because there was only fifteen of them made. I slipped into a Lamborghini and drove that too but Danny was hilarious – they wanted rock 'n' roll and we did warn them.'

Danny's drunken behaviour with Hassan has regularly landed him in hot water with Joanne. Hassan revealed, 'My wife loves him, his wife hates me.'

Their bond became more than just friendship when Tamer gave Danny a novel present for Xmas – a chance to be a chairman of a football club. Tamer was chairman of amateur football club Greenwich Borough FC but decided to become President, leaving room for Danny to join in 2007. While the present was a thoughtful one from Tamer, he did have an ulterior motive. 'He is very excited about it. Danny wants to do everything he can to help the club and, hopefully, his involvement will attract a few more female fans to watch us play!'

If his fans thought the role of chairman was an odd one for Danny to tackle, he admitted he struggled with the idea as well. In an interview with *Sky Sports*, he said, 'I'm going to hold my hands up. He's put it on me, this chairman thing. I know nothing about being a chairman. I can just about tie my shoelaces, let alone start running a club!'

However, he told *NewsShopper* that he would take the role seriously. 'I have always been interested in Greenwich Borough because Tamer has been there for a long time. I've played in a few charity games there before and seen quite a few matches already, so you could say I have a bit of a soft spot for them. As soon as Tamer asked me to become chairman, I just knew it was something I had to say yes to. I just love football and the chance of being involved with a club is like a dream come true.'

Football has obviously played a huge part in his life and he is a keen footballer as well, having played a number of celeb football games for charity. However, because of his fame he can't really be seen on the Sunday pitches any more, as 'the opposing centre half might want to spend the game asking me questions and interviewing me'. Or even worse. 'I used to play Sunday league football but, since I started getting famous, people want to break my legs.'

Also, he's not as fit as he used to be. 'I'm not a bad footballer but I've got the lungs of a sixty-year-old because all the smoking and drugs have taken their toll on me,' he told the *Guardian*.

While Danny was thankful for Hassan giving him the sporting opportunity, he wasn't best pleased when he was forced to wear a Millwall shirt for the cause. Hassan recounted the tale. 'There was this charity event at my football club, Greenwich Borough. There's this friend of mine who had a son who was terminally ill and we had to get him over to Mexico for this special treatment, and we held an auction event where my good friend Danny Dyer comes over to lend his support. As part of the auction we've put in a signed Millwall shirt and someone's bid £500 for it on a condition that Danny Dyer wears it. Well, Danny's shoulders slumped and he looked at me. I said, "Danny, the kids dying and a monkey [£500] is a monkey, mate, so you've got to put it on. He's put this Millwall shirt on and, poor Dan's face. I did feel sorry for him because he is an avid West Ham supporter who even draws the crossed hammers when signing his name. So he's standing there in the middle of the clubhouse, with his shoulders sunk down and, as everyone's taking pictures, he's looking at me with venom in his eyes.'

But Danny got his own back not long after. 'Danny Dyer set me up,' recalled Hassan in a 2007 interview with Cass Pennant. 'This Premiership All-Stars tournament involved Sky TV and I didn't know anything about it. So Danny's gone to me, "Listen, we're playing this charity Premiership All-Stars thing and I've put your name up so do you want to play?" And I said, "Yeah, fine." As it got closer, I got this call from the producer saying that I was playing for West Ham. I immediately said, "Oh, really, can't I play for Chelsea? I know a few players down there," and they said, "No, no, you're only playing for West Ham, that's the only space that there is." So I said, "Who's in the team then?" and it was Danny Dyer, Geoff Bell, [Frank] McAvennie and all the boys, so I thought, All right, sweet. Geoff Bell's Millwall. And Danny's on the phone, [saying,] "Come on, Tam, do it for me, do it for this." OK, fine, until I got there and seen it's a massive West Ham fest, as all their fans appear to have completely taken over the stadium.'

The West Ham fans then promptly proceeded to boo his every touch, knowing that Hassan was a Millwall fan, much to Danny's delight.

For his next project Danny moved from the directors' box to being an agent – in an all-star TV movie called *All in the Game*. Not only did it reunite Danny with his cinematic sporting pastime, he also got to star with his all-time idol – Ray Winstone.

'It was a dream for me. He's one of the idols, one of the reasons I started acting. So it was a big moment,' beamed Danny.

After his first audition, he was called back in and things looked very good indeed. While Danny was overjoyed at being able to work with his idol, there was a catch. And for the heartthrob, it was a pretty big catch.

'They said, "We want to give you a different look. When Ray was younger he had ginger hair and Ray thinks that it's a good idea." And I thought, For fucks sake, can't I go blonde? "No, it's got to be ginger." Ah, fuck it, I'll do it. I want to work with Ray; I'll do whatever it takes. So I go get my hair dyed ginger and, I've got to say, it was horrible, fucking horrible. The thing is, I've got to work with Ray.'

But it was to get worse. When he went back to the producers, he was told he had to have his eyebrows dyed ginger as well. 'Even ginger people don't have ginger eyebrows. I had to put a fucking stop to that. Ginger fucking eyebrows!'

However, he got a shock when he proudly showed his new look to his idol. Recalling the moment to Channel Bee, Danny comments, 'The first thing he says to me was, "What have you done to your hair, you ginger cunt?" I was absolutely devastated. I thought he was going to go, "Well done, boy, I see what you're doing. Trying to change a bit." But he goes, "You've got to be fucking stupid, don't you?"'

Yet it was to get even worse for the now flame-haired actor. On set, he was called 'ginger cunt' constantly by his idol, and off set he had to endure wisecracks whenever he went to his local. He recalled, 'I found myself going to the boozers and saying, "I've done it for a part. Let's get it out of the way and then crack on, have a booze."'

But in all seriousness, Danny was simply overjoyed to be working with Winstone. Four days into the shoot, he told his fans via a video interview, 'I fucking love him. It's a fucking joy to finally work with him. All my dreams come true. I'm standing with him, he likes me and he knows me. We haven't done our big scenes yet but I can't wait. I want to shine in front of him. I want him to say, "Oh, he's got something, this kid." He's great, very professional, very funny.

'He's playing my dad. It doesn't get any fucking better, I tell you. Fuck Pacino, fuck De Niro, I'm working with Ray Winstone.'

It's easy to see why Danny looks up to Winstone. Not only do they both come from the East End and primarily make British films, but Winstone's CV is a strong one, filled with films in which he had unwavering self-belief, a trait that Danny definitely admires.

In an interview with the *Guardian*, Winstone said, 'If it does something to me when I read it, makes me cry, or makes me laugh, I'll go with it. But if I don't like it, no matter what the offer is, I won't do it. And I was like that even when I was out of work too. I think maybe that's part of the embarrassment of being the kid who goes to the pictures or watches television, and I think, My mates wouldn't like that, or my dad wouldn't like that, because I had an audience in mind. And you find a kind of honesty in that.'

Written by Tony Grounds, *All in the Game* was a scathing look at the modern English game. The idea for the screenplay came when his football friends began to constantly ask the same questions. – 'Why are the footballers paid so much?' and 'What form of parasite is the football agent?' Grounds told *The Times*, 'Football is now centred on the elite top twenty clubs. Back when *Match of the Day* first bought rights to show games, they paid £5,000, which was distributed between ninety-two clubs. Now the latest figure is £2 billion to be divided between the top twenty and the rest can go to hell.'

It tells the story of Frankie (Winstone), a corrupt and wildly fearsome Premiership manager of a club that is flirting with relegation. Things look worse when Frankie's underhand agent son Martin (Dyer) tries to sell the club's star player under the club's nose – a move which would guarantee a lot of money for him and his dad. 'I play a right snake in this. I play a football agent, and not a very nice one,' he told his fans.

As Grounds said, 'I don't expect many of the top clubs to like what they see.' You can see why Tony's original idea for the title was *Sweet FA*. However, Grounds insists Frankie isn't based on anyone in real life. 'It genuinely isn't anyone's story. You'd be sued if you named names – nobody's ever got any proof. The sums are now so colossal that it's not brown envelopes, it's offshore accounts.'

Winstone added in a *Radio Times* interview, 'Quite a well-known coach and a great player told me that, when young players come to these clubs, they ask them a question: "Why do you want to be a footballer?" Ninety-nine times out of a hundred they want the jewellery, the car and the girl. The one that really affected him was the one who said, "I want to score the winning goal in the Cup Final," and the coach said he'd take that player over anyone else, but he also said that they're few and far between.'

Since the film has been aired, however, Danny has been noticing some unpleasant side effects. He believes the ginger dye has caused his hair to recede. 'I couldn't get it out of my hair. It took me six months. I couldn't fucking get it out. I kept washing it. I think I started losing my wig after that. I'm receding a bit but it only started after I dyed it. If the worst comes to the worst, I'll sue,' he joked. 'It's down to Channel 4 I'm losing my canister.'

But it seems it was worth it to work with his idol. 'I'd

have been an extra on anything just to be around him [Winstone]. Mixed emotions – got to work with Ray but, at the same time, he was giving me grief every day. And he wasn't even ginger when he was a kid!'

Chapter Sixteen

Laughing his Head Off

I knew the pressure was on me and I'd have to deliver

The *Football Factory* and *The Business* were massive hits for Danny that secured him a sizeable fan base. It was a lucrative niche but Danny was desperate to show his comedy talents. And so he signed on to appear in horror comedy *Severance*.

Although it seems Danny was reluctant at first because the horror movies he had seen in recent years were 'run of the mill', in *Severance* he saw a chance to do something different with the genre – a genre he was a fan of.

Talking to *Time Out*, Danny said, 'I've been sent horror before and they've been shit. You know, "Let's start killing people. Let's get to the scary bit." It's a hard thing to pull off because it's such an obvious genre, so it's great to find something like this which is different. When I read this, I thought, Wow, wow, wow, why ain't they offering me this? It was one of those auditions you go into and think, I've got to get this job. You get those rarely.'

The script he read was vastly different to the writer James Moran's original script, entitled *P45*, which focused on a group of interns fending off a crazed psychopath. It turns out, however, that it was set up by the company who orchestrated a 'whoever survives is promoted' motto.

Severance director Chris Smith recalled, 'The original writer, James Moran, came up with the idea. He was travelling home from work one day on the tube and there was a bunch of stockbrokers all around him, drunk on a Friday night, and he thought, I'm gonna go home and kill some yuppies. He literally got home and started writing. It was his first ever script.

'I loved what James had done in his screenplay though. He took seven characters you got to really like in both a human and humorous way before turning the tables and killing them nastily. Some of the humour was broader than my usual taste so I worked with the writer to make the story into something more ironic, more based on truth. That way you could empathise with the characters as well as be scared along with them when they eventually died,' added Smith, on the film's production notes.

'I inserted new twists and turns and put some more girls in the character mix, plus new angles on what was scaring me at that time. For one, the idea that the arms industry had power without responsibility. Those sorts of themes were necessary texture to make the plot darker and bleaker, and about much more than just having your job at stake. I thought the title *Severance* was ideal, reminiscent of *Deliverance* but with a sharp, witty edge.'

As soon as Danny read the script, he knew he wanted to

play the character of Steve, the roguish computer whiz kid of arms company Palisade Defence. More importantly, so did the director, Chris Smith.

'For me, Danny was the only guy who could play the Steve character right from the start,' recalled Smith. 'And what happens is they give you names and all the money people have got their ideas as to who they think is funny or right for the part. And they didn't think Danny would be funny enough. They thought he was a straight actor so I asked them if they'd actually seen his comic timing in *Human Traffic* or *The Football Factory*. I wanted straight actors who could be funny.'

Danny revealed in an interview with *Film Review*, 'The Steve part blew me away. I knew I could shine in *Severance*. And I knew I nailed it after a couple of readings. Chris clearly loved my audition because he bounced around like a lunatic.'

In a 2006 interview with *Total Film*, Smith said, 'As soon as I met him I found he's a really loveable guy; he's the one who'll tell the jokes and get the vibe going. He's very much acting when he's playing a thug – he's not a thug, he's a cheeky little boy and so I tried to get as much of that into this character as possible.'

Their relationship was to be a close one – and, like Danny's relationship with Love, it came about because Smith took a risk to cast Danny. When it comes to filmmaking, Danny seems to prize loyalty over everything else. If someone has put their faith in him, he will do everything he can to repay it in full.

He told *Film Focus*, 'Chris Smith wanted me but the

financiers didn't, for whatever reason. I was under pressure immediately because they thought I wasn't funny enough. I've got a bit of a bad-boy image and they just didn't want me in the film. Chris had to fight, fight, fight so that, when they finally gave him the OK to put me in, I knew the pressure was on me and I'd have to deliver. But all that does is make me raise my game, really.'

Like Danny, Smith saw the film as a chance to show people that there was more to him than they might have first thought. His 2004 debut *Creep*, about a deformed killer stalking a woman who has been locked in on the London Underground, was met with mixed reviews. 'He learned from *Creep*,' explained Danny. 'He didn't make *Creep* the way he wanted to make it exactly – he had to cut a few corners and was definitely a "yes man" on *Creep*. He wasn't that on *Severance*. He would have arguments when he didn't get things exactly right.'

Smith admitted, 'What I learned from *Creep* was to involve the actors more and put my hand up when I was wrong about something. Here, I took my seven lead actors into the deep end and learned everything I could about their personalities and how they viewed their characters. Very soon it was an eight-man team, completely aware of what each was doing every second of the day. That's why I end *Severance* with an homage to *The Deer Hunter*. You have taken a thrill ride with these seven great characters through their petty squabbles, camaraderie, laughter, spooky stories and, hopefully, upsetting deaths. So I show them again over the final credits. As each actor's credit comes up, we play a single joyous moment from the movie for each of them and freeze frame on their smile. They appear in the order they died: Harris, Jill, Gordon, Billy, Richard... then Maggie and Steve. It's a warm reminder of their engaging moments and should send the audience out on a high. I want them to think about the characters they've enjoyed spending time with as much as I enjoyed putting them in the direst jeopardy.'

As with Love, Danny was able and welcome to add his input into the filming process, something which Danny was quick to seize upon, making suggestions that some of the film's humour at the its later stages be dropped because it undercut the film's sense of danger.

Speaking about the director, Danny added, 'His energy is amazing and he's gotten the best out of me like no one else has before.'

His energy was needed as it was to be an eventful shoot, particularly with the language differences among the Hungarian special-effects and stunt teams. In the documentary of the British DVD release, Smith is regularly seen exasperated with the key pyrotechnician Attila Torok and special-effects supervisor Jozsef Gerencser when fire stunts wouldn't work, guns wouldn't fire and the missile launcher fired the wrong way.

One scene required Laura Harris to hit one of the soldiers with a rock. Smith recalled, 'I told them the size I wanted and they came back with a stone – a hard stone, perfectly the size I wanted – the same but hard. So they had made a stone out of fibreglass. I said, "What's that?" and he said, "It's a stone." "What do I do with it?" "Put it on the floor." And I was like, "Put it on the floor? There are stones everywhere. I want to hit someone over the head with it!"'

Even one of the film's biggest action stunts wasn't safe for the Hungarian stunt team's eccentricities. The scene when the bush crashes and flips on to its side is spectacular – almost too spectacular. Once the cameras rolled, the stuntman decided to do it at 55mph rather than the 35mph as planned. While the stuntman managed to knock himself out in the process, the stunt was so good that Smith had to add more bloody make-up to the cast because they needed to look more injured.

Smith recalled of the incident, 'The coach was our shark from *Jaws*. It broke down every day but I knew for the drama to be effective it had to be done filmed on a coach for real rather than studio controlled. Our Hungarian stunt driver, who also plays the coach driver in the film, really went for it too – he flew over the ramp at 50mph and was unconscious when the paramedics went in. Because the crash looked so much more impressive than I had envisioned, we had to make the actors look more injured as a result. So Toby Stephens had his stomach split open and Claudie Blakley's skull was caked in glass and blood, adding more credibility to the reason she wanders off dazed into the woods.'

The eight-week shoot, starring Danny, Laura Harris, Tim McInnerny, Toby Stephens, Claudie Blakley, Andy Nyman and Babou Ceesay, was split between Hungary and the Isle of Man. Labelled as '*The Office* meets *Deliverance*', the film focuses on the European Sales division of weapons company Palisade Defence heading out for a team-building weekend in Hungary. However, when their bus breaks down, they are forced to shelter in a rundown loft. But office politics, bickering and flirting come second to staying alive when unseen forces hunt them.

The film's producer Jason Newark was convinced they had a hit on their hands. 'One of Chris's greatest strengths is his characters. When you have an ensemble of characters in a horror film, the biggest mistake is making them too similar. That was a danger Chris avoided by separating each character out, both on the page and eventually in casting. He honed in on their differences while making ample room for key interaction. That has been one of the most satisfying parts of the whole *Severance* experience.'

And Newark was understandably thrilled with his cast. 'We spent four months finding the perfect people for the parts. By that I mean actors who would perfectly embody their characters by bringing many of their own personal qualities to the parts. We drove our casting director Gail Stevens mad with our fussiness. We could never see enough people, or make enough suggestions from her copious lists. It took us absolutely ages to put our cast together because we needed especially gifted actors who could bring the comedy elements alive while inhabiting the horror space. This genre needs great actors to let go sufficiently to first invite the audience in and then make them scared for their lives. Chris was adamant about pushing every actor to the screaming limit so they could show their range. They had to go there and be convincing or else the film's integrity would suffer.

'We both loved Danny Dyer in *The Football Factory*.

He's totally down to earth and has an infectious and roguish charm that has provided him with a broad fan base. Men respect his cheekiness as much as women respond to his sex-symbol status. He showed a great grasp of natural comedy in *Human Traffic* and clearly could be the life and soul of any party. Here, he wraps up all the different bits of what we wanted to come together from his past films for the role of Steve.'

Following the huge success of *Shaun of the Dead*, it wasn't long before a raft of films appeared attempting to replicate the film's blend of comedy horror. Unlike films such as *Shrooms* or *The Cottage*, *Severance* is primarily horror, but with added quirks and real-life humour thrown in.

Smith said in the film's production notes, 'In the horror genre, everyone has seen everything. So, if you can surprise an audience with some ingenuity, they love you for it. I approached every scene in *Severance* with the attitude: OK, what's the best I can do? How can I kill this character spectacularly in a way that matches their personality? Harris's death scene is a case in point. Talking with Jill about the guillotine, he entertains her with the little-known fact that, even when the head is severed from the body, the brain can still think for a few minutes. When Harris meets his fate and is beheaded, I show him looking at his own body a few yards away with an expression of "I told you so". Each character has been fully developed so by the time their deaths come they can have their own imaginative and shocking moment in the sun.

'But it's not a horror comedy in the traditional sense, like *Scary Movie* or *Shaun of the Dead*,' continues Smith.

'My motivation in making *Severance* was to further explore the areas of *Creep* that really interested me. When I took *Creep* on the international fantasy festival circuit, I was intrigued to note audiences always responded most to the set-piece moments of mischievous horror, like the gynaecological torture scene. My aim with *Severance* is to prove that you can be continually playful within a non-one-liner context, yet still provide the big scares and grisly horror. It's all down to a balance of fun grimness mixed with cliché conventions. Funny things happen but it isn't a sit-com, the characters aren't telling jokes. Horrific things happen but *Severance* isn't just about extreme splatter either. The tone is pure gallows humour. You know from the get-go you are meant to laugh. It begins with two girls stripping off as a strung-up victim gets knifed. In the second half, Steve tries to stuff Gordon's severed foot into the coach fridge. That sums up the entire atmosphere – real life getting in the way of the chilling craziness and being played dead straight.'

Steve is not your typical action hero. He's your normal run-of-the-mill twenty-something male caught up in an extraordinary situation – thus, rather than make cool heroic quips, he hides in a cupboard. Instead of executing perfect martial-art moves, he bites his way through fights and he will use any mind-altering substance that comes to hand in a bid to mask the deadly situation he faces. Steve is what many people see as the typical Danny Dyer character – a cocky and roguish Jack-the-lad who takes drugs and is women obsessed. We first see Danny in the film attempting to hire an escort for the weekend on the website balklandbabes.com. When forced to hole up in the derelict cottage, Dyer spends the first half-an-hour high on magic mushrooms.

What the majority of Danny's films hold is a sort of wish fulfilment (a 'you lucky bastard' kind of thing) for his fans. And *Severance* keeps up with that tradition near the end, as a worse-for-wear Danny comes to the rescue of two Eastern European escorts who have been shorn of most of their clothes after stringing most of their garments together to make a rope (at least the screenwriter made a narrative attempt for getting the girls out of their clothes!), although even Smith was impressed at how the girls got to be near nude.

The film also features an ending that only Danny could get away with. Bloodied, battered and bruised, he escapes with Laura Harris and the two European prostitutes. The memorable last line has Danny cheekily querying, 'Foursome?'

But, before shooting started, the cast got a shock when they arrived at the hotel a day before filming in the Hungarian forest. There was a typed note saying, 'Tick alert – you will be filming in a forest where the ticks are vicious. Tuck your trousers into your socks and check your pubic hair. Get others to help you.'

It was a situation that could have proved more serious for Danny, who once again had to strip off. This time he goes to the toilet in the woods. In the commentary for the film, he recalled, 'It's a weird scene to be in – with your cock hanging out is a mad fucking thing in the forest.' Luckily, for Danny's sake, there were no ticks around that day!

One scene sees Danny indulging in a company team-building exercise of paintball, although it seems he wasn't in possession of the paintball gun that often. 'In between the shots, I wasn't allowed to hold the paintball gun for some reason. There was always someone rushing up to take it from me.'

Another scene that no doubt held interest for Danny when he read the script was a fantasy sequence in which Steve believes the lodge they are hiding in once housed nymphomaniac lesbian nurses who pamper and grope the new male doctor, played, of course, by Danny.

Despite it being another early morning call (6.30am), Danny was up in plenty of time that day. 'What a great day that was,' he recalled. 'I think I was up since 4.30am waiting to be picked up. I was showered nice and early – ready for the day ahead. It went a bit quick for me but it was mad being surrounded by all these birds. It was a beautiful thing.'

Severance was also a chance for Danny to be reacquainted with Hungary – a place where he filmed as a seventeen-year-old in *Cadfael*. And he was just as unimpressed the second time. 'I couldn't wait to leave it. I didn't think I would ever, ever find myself saying, "I can't wait to get to the Isle of Man," but I did say that a few times.'

Away from the film world, London was attacked by terrorists on 7 July 2005. And Danny, who is for ever associated with the city that he was born in, was filming *Severance* thousands of miles away when the tragedy happened, although he felt it deeply.

'While we were shooting it, it was the time of the London bombings. Which was pretty fucking heavy. I mean, I live in London, I've always lived in London, all my family live in London. We filmed it in Hungary and, when the news came through that that there had been fucking bombs on trains, it really fucking upset me! I wanted to just go home, you know? I lost all hope for doing the film. But obviously I calmed down after a few hours. So that was pretty heavy.'

Smith added, 'Danny, for example, all his family and everyone he knows lives in London, so things like that suddenly make you feel privileged to have this life.'

Since the bombings, Danny has become more protective of his kids. 'I'm not really a violent man. I'll swerve violence. I fear for my daughter who is now eleven. I don't let her play outside. I keep her in my house all the time. But I do fear for her. And the fact that we are at war at the moment. She knows all about that. She knows about the bombs going off on trains and asks me questions like, "They aren't going to bomb me, Daddy, are they?"'

But it seems the tragic events only made the cast bond even more.

'It was a joy. None of us knew each other before, but this is filmmaking, you all get thrown in together, go away for eight weeks in the middle of nowhere and you're all a team fighting the same battle. You don't always necessarily get on with everyone, but on this we did,' insisted Danny.

However, Danny was, in fact, worried whether or not he would hit it off with one cast member in particular. He feared that maybe he and Shakespearean actor Toby Stephens would 'hate each other'. 'We've made such totally different films that you just wouldn't think it would work,' he said.

Fortunately, Danny's fears were unfounded and the two got on famously, although Smith joked to *Time Out*, 'We were laughing about the fact that the only other way you could see those together is if Toby was the landowner on horseback and Danny turns up as the postman or the gamekeeper.'

As for Danny, the horror genre was a new one for Stephens. 'I'd never done a horror film before and that's why I wanted to make *Severance*. It was a cracking read. It starts off as something funny and then does a hairpin turn into grisly terror. It's a mould breaker in that it veers from comedy to horror without it being easily categorised as a comedy or horror film. My father [acclaimed actor Sir Robert Stephens] made a twisted and strange British horror movie in 1973 titled *The Asphyx* and I feel this fits that mould too, with its endearing penchant for oblique weirdness.

'Harris is the best weapons salesman Palisade has got. He's arrogant, brash and knows he's invaluable to the company, which puts him in direct confrontation with his boss Richard. They are constantly at loggerheads because Harris knows he's better equipped for Richard's job. That's what is so good about the *Severance* set-up. You immediately see the internecine battles and political power struggles within the European office division. None of them really like each other and that's what makes the story so unsettling from the beginning. They are clearly going to get into trouble and, when they do, what's going to happen? Who can they rely on when each one is a vicious backstabber?'

There was one moment in particular that tickled Danny. During the scene where he gives Andy Nyman's character (who has just lost one of his legs) some Ecstasy to take away the pain, Danny thought he should give the clean-living actor some much-needed advice how to act while on drugs.

'Andy wasn't too happy about that. I said, "This is what you do, you haven't had any before." He's said, "I've never had my fucking legs chopped off either, have I?" I was like, "All right," and so I skulked off back into the shadows. Fair enough.'

Danny even had an admirer on set. Actress Laura Harris admits she was quite smitten with Danny, although she struggled to cope with his accent. She told the *Mirror*, 'He's an absolute doll. He's just pure instinct, which I love, and his instincts are awesome – although I did have to become accustomed to what he was saying because of his accent. He would also be using this phrasing and I had no idea what he was saying. I just didn't get the cockney rhyming slang at all.'

Smith joked, 'I don't want anyone calling Laura Harris the token American. She's the token Canadian. David Gilliam, who plays George, is the token American. I saw Laura in *The Faculty*, *24* and *Dead Like Me*, and thought she exuded a unique survival quality. She's someone you just know is going to try and make it somehow. Laura as

Maggie is my ironical Sigourney Weaver/*Alien* type who will do her best to defeat the odds whatever it takes.'

Describing her character, Harris said, 'Maggie is from mid-America, Michael Moore's USA. She wanted to get the hell out of Dodge, and what she knows about the most is guns, the reason she joins Palisade. Maggie comes into her own during the final stages because girls from her area know how to shoot a gun. Just go to any range in, say, Michigan and the American right to bear arms will be on full display.'

Harris, who played terrorist Marie Warner in the second series of *24*, grew up in Vancouver but headed to LA with 'five hundred bucks and no green card' to be with her boyfriend at the time.

She added of Danny to the *Observer*, 'I'm not the sex in *Severance*. Danny Dyer is. I love him. I told him he's the kind of guy I'd have slept with ten years ago, but now I've learned from my mistakes!'

Smith was getting the best out of Danny and, as with director Nick Love, it was to do with tough love. 'Sometimes you just need a pat on the bum, others need to be bollocked. What Chris did with me was wind me up. I'd do a take and he'd say, "That's perfect, now I want you to do it like this." I'd be like, "Come on then, you're wrong but let's do it." But he'd get the right performance out of me. I didn't realise it at the time but that was his way of dealing with me and it helped me.'

As Danny told *Film Focus*, Smith's most appealing trait in directing actors was his childish enthusiasm. '[He's] like a kid in a sweet shop. He's like a little boy who can't believe he's directing. So you follow Chris because you want to do well for him. He's so passionate and so excited about being a director.'

For the gruelling fight sequence, Chris told Danny that he wanted his character to fight like a hooligan, to fight like any man in a pub would if his life depended on it. Not that Danny needed the motivation. He threw himself into the fight scene, where his character has to fend off two of the soldiers. 'It was tough, I must say. I took a few beatings. I gave as good as I got, I tell you. The stuntmen were holding their backs in pain afterwards. I was thinking, Fucking hell, I'm going to feel this tomorrow. I loved being beaten up, because the more bruised, bloodied and dirty I got, the more it put me in the right mood for the killing scenes.'

As with his experience on *The Business*, where he would completely segue into his character Frankie whenever he went into costume, the same thing happened in *Severance* – but it would be make-up this time.

The film's hair and make-up designer Jan Sewell explained, 'He gets head-butted, his tooth falls out and his eye swells to the size of a golf ball. I made a dental cast that allowed us to give the illusion of broken teeth and the eye was a gelatine appliance. The latter gave Danny less and less vision the more he got beaten up and hit in the face. Danny found it invigorating, and the more we bruised him up and dirtied him down, the more he got into the mood for the scene. You could see his whole demeanour change during the 45-minute application.'

Danny had to train hard for those fight scenes, and for

the first time he had to have a personal trainer. For the beer-guzzling boy from the East End, that was something of a shock. He told *Indie London*, 'The part needed it. I did six weeks with a personal trainer, three days a week, cut down on my food. He basically wanted definition. The terrorists in this film are horrible – they're big men, so, for me to turn around and fight them, I had to make it look believable. But it was knackering as well. That fighting scene was two days, twelve hours a day. I like a smoke and I like a booze but I was in shape for this because I did the gym thing first. You're drained afterwards.' And he was drained long after the cameras stopped rolling. 'I lost loads of weight and I'm still exhausted from it because I did my own stunts. I didn't learn until later I could have had a stuntman!' he added in a 2005 interview with the *Mirror*. 'I wasn't allowed to eat potatoes or the skin off chicken. I did as I was told because it was for the job, and I did feel healthy at the end of it.'

Arguably the film's standout funniest scene features just Danny trying to jam a prosthetic severed leg into a mini fridge. And it's one that he knew he could make a success. 'I'm quite an instinctive actor. I know how I'm going to play it. I didn't want to milk it too much, just try and jam it in, get the bottles out, take the shoe, then the sock off – and the foot looked so real, it was horrendous. They took a real cast of his foot, toenails and everything, hairy toes ... and it was very heavy. What a scene to play as an actor.'

However, it's one scene Smith had to fight to keep in. He revealed, 'They said to me, "You might not need that scene." I said, "What do you mean? That's one of the best scenes in the film." They thought that, as long as Danny's character says later in the movie that he's put the foot in the fridge, you don't actually need to see him put it in there.' Fearing that the scene would be cut before they actually shot it, he quickly tried to get the shot in the can. Unfortunately for Danny, it was the day after his birthday and he was rather worse for wear. 'He is still fucking wasted,' recalled Smith. 'He's had about a quarter of an hour's sleep. He comes in, does two takes, and it was brilliant. He went straight home.' No doubt straight to bed!

Smith was delighted with the final product, saying, 'Shooting *Severance* went better than I ever expected. Steve tripping works so well thanks to Danny Dyer nailing the tone perfectly. We had a bear strut across the road in Hungary, stare at the camera and saunter on. You couldn't have planned it any better.

While the film never did find the audience it probably deserved on the big screen, it has definitely thrived through word of mouth and has become a cult hit on DVD.

The majority of the reviews were kind to Danny, with the *Telegraph* saying the 'pick of the cast is the leading man, Danny Dyer, who is fast becoming British cinema's cuddly chav of choice'. Like the review says, 'It is certainly hard to imagine anyone else firing off this classic, nay Wildean, encomium to English ladyfolk – "You buy them a Bacardi Breezer and they'll ride you like Seabiscuit" – with quite such scuzzy authority.'

After filming, Danny was in a great place. He believed he

was finally getting the kudos he deserved. 'I've been offered a film called *The Lesbian Vampire Killers* but I'm in two minds over what I want to do next. [That film was later made in 2009, starring *Gavin and Stacey*'s James Corden and Matthew Horne, and was savaged by critics.] I'm actually at a stage at the moment where I don't have to audition and it's freaking me out a little bit, to be honest. I love it but I'm not used to it.'

While things looked good, with Danny being Danny, the focus would soon be on something other than acting.

Chapter Seventeen
Danny's Dyerbolical Mouth

I always put my foot in it

While his performance in *Severance* was gaining positive reviews for Danny, most of the headlines around that time were in the gossip rather than the film-critic section because, once again, Danny's big mouth had got him in trouble. He landed in hot water after some unfavourable remarks about one of the shooting locations for *Severance*. Talking to Irish magazine *Hot Press*, he said, 'Bloody Isle of Man. What a fucked-up place. There are lots of horrible little towns where everyone looks like they've been doing their cousins for generations. Then, when you get into the woods, there are waterfalls and some really untouched land, but it was a lot more eerie than I thought it would be.'

Danny had to print an apology after the citizens of the Isle of Man understandably took offence at the remark. 'I've got to retract that statement. I've upset them all. I do tend to open my mouth a little bit. I said that they all fuck each other, which isn't very nice. I didn't mean it. They're all right, the Isle of Man. It's a crazy little place but they're very proud of their rock. They make a lot of films there; they're good to the film game. I was just a bit homesick.'

It was not the first time Danny's mouth would land him in trouble. In 2005, frustrated at his peers' Hollywood success, he fired a withering rant at a series of British actors, saying, 'I always thought that money came with fame but it has not happened like that for me. There is a certain group of actors, like Ewan McGregor, Orlando Bloom – all those cunts – that earn all the fucking millions, and the rest of us scrabble around for bits and bobs. For *The Football Factory* I was on five hundred quid a week. For a six-week shoot I got three grand and that goes fucking nowhere. I've got money coming from DVD sales but that's got to be carved up and that takes for ever.'

It wasn't his last swipe at Bloom. 'I do genuinely think Orlando Bloom is a cunt. I've never met him but he's in the same game as me and he's loaded. I get a bit bitter, to be honest. I'm still living in the ghetto in East London and he's earning three million quid a film. He got lucky. He came out of drama school and got *Lord of the Rings* and then goes and gets another trilogy, *Pirates of the Caribbean*. He wasn't all that good in it but it put him on the map, didn't it? He's the opposite of me; he's well media trained and boring. Plus he can't act. And to me, that's quite an important thing for an actor,' he said in 2008. There was even another rant, this time to *The London Paper*. 'He's got all sorts of dough, loads of screaming girls chasing him, but he hasn't honed his craft yet, he's a rubbish actor. I don't think anybody I've ever come across has said, "You know what, he's a great actor, that Orlando Bloom." He's got a good name; I think that's what it is. And quite an irritating face.' And one more for good measure. 'I just can't stand Orlando Bloom. I can't. I just want to get his face and fucking squeeze it.'

Here are some of his other greatest hits:

On Victoria Beckham: 'I think skinny birds need a fucking Big Mac meal and some chicken nuggets.'

On Madonna: 'I think how much she charges for a concert is a fucking joke.'

On James McAvoy: 'He's absolutely gone flying. Bafta nominations, presenting at the Oscars... Why? Because he's running about with a floppy hairdo and he does period dramas.'

However, there are times when Danny knows he's gone too far and concedes that's he's too open for his own good. Talking to *Zoo* magazine in 2008, he said, 'I realised it makes me look a cunt. I'd said McAvoy has only got where he is because he wears a floppy wig and bowls about with a mad accent – but I was only fucking about. That is the problem with me doing the press sometimes when I'm in a right hump. I had a big barney with the missus. She wound me up and I went into an interview and someone asked me about McAvoy.'

He reportedly also had to apologise to Guy Ritchie after launching another tirade at his then wife Madonna. 'I wouldn't pay £150 to watch Madonna, no way. I used to love her. She was the first person that ever made me hot, but she's over.'

The *Daily Star* reported that Ritchie was furious. A source told the paper, 'Guy can take the rough and tumble with the lads. He knows just what Danny's sense of humour is and he can take it. Even Madonna is able to handle a raucous wit but that was too much. Danny and Guy know each other from the Britpack scene and they've always got on well, so Dan was happy to apologise for any offence taken.'

The apologies didn't stop there. Next up was Boy George, although it did make Danny realise that maybe he should think about what he says first. 'I've learned not to shoot my mouth off. I called Boy George a lump and he wrote to me saying how much it hurt. It made me feel fucking small. I've had media training.'

The training seemed to work – at first anyway. After telling the *Daily Star* that he hates media parties, he launched into a rant at Jay Kay. 'That Jamiroquai geezer. You can't go to parties like that and not expect to have your fucking picture taken, and then hit out at photographers. What a dick. Sorry about that. But when something makes me angry I can't help myself.'

When he was asked about his hurtful remarks to Madonna, he said, 'I fucking love her. She was my first love. I wanked over her picture. But now she's almost fifty... [he stops himself] See, I've learned.'

Not only did his rants hurt people but they also cost him a lucrative role on stage. Danny was in talks to play Bill Sykes in the big-budget West End production of

Oliver alongside whichever actress won the BBC reality show *I'll Do Anything*. It would have been a lucrative career move, as it was bound to be a hugely successful affair with Rowan Atkinson playing Fagin. However, the thought of singing was giving Danny sleepless nights. 'The producers approached me and offered me the role of Sykes but I'm terrified about singing on stage. Luckily, I'll only have to sing one song.'

He originally stayed secretive over the reasons for his failure to get the part, telling a newspaper, 'It's a bit gutting really. I just got the call; I was down to the last two.'

However, he admitted all to Radio 1 soon after. 'I opened my mouth a little and I should have kept my mouth shut. I'm gutted about that. You live and learn on those things. I'd had a few lagers, spoke to a journalist and ruined my chances of playing Bill Sykes. It's a real shame and I won't be doing it again.'

In an interview with Charlotte Church, he added, 'I didn't have a pop at Ewan McGregor. I've got no problem with him at all. Basically, I got asked a question: "Am I a millionaire because I'm a fucking actor?" And I said, "Am I fuck. Ewan McGregor and Orlando Bloom and all them cunts earn the money. The rest of us just scratch about." I think Ewan's a good actor. I don't get Bloom, but, listen, I'm learning to just shut your fucking mouth. Don't slag people off because it makes you look muggy.'

A noble sentiment but one that Danny doesn't seem able to stick to. He was at it again in 2009, having a verbal dig at *Gavin & Stacey*'s Matthew Horne. 'Matthew Horne is one of the worst actors I've ever seen in my life. He's just got nothing about him, the geezer. No substance and no depth. It annoys me that no one's clocked that.'

Considering that Horne was suffering the worst reviews of his career from both his TV sketch show with James Corden and their comedy horror film *Lesbian Vampire Killers* – and he had collapsed on stage not long before – it was definitely a case of kicking a man when he's down.

But for now Danny was flying high, and next up was another film with Nick Love.

Chapter Eighteen

Outlaw

It's probably easier for these kids to buy guns than cigarettes

Love's next film was to be his most controversial since *The Football Factory*. He said, 'The theme is Blair's legacy in a way – it's like Middle England turning on each other. There is so much happening at the moment; you don't even need to get past three pages in the paper at the moment. You open the *Sun* and it's there before you get to the tits!

'I have to say, like most people, when Blair got into power a few years ago I was enthusiastic about it. I felt like the Tories were dreadful great grey bores and Blair was dynamic. I felt that he was going to do some amazing stuff in this country because I felt he was listening to the man on the street,' he told *Indie London*. 'But ten years later, I don't know if we've regressed but we've certainly stagnated. We haven't made any forward progress.'

As had happened before, Love disappeared off the face of the earth, with Danny not having a clue when he would come back or what he would come back with. Asked on his website whether he would be working with Love again, he said, 'All I know is he's writing a film called *Outlaw*. I won't see him for a while, as he goes off and writes and shoots squirrels in the country. I haven't seen him yet about it. I don't know if he will pick me for this. Of course, it will fucking hurt if he doesn't because I love working with him. All I know is that he wants to do something different. He's done all he wants with the London thing. He wanted to make a film about young kids on a London council estate, he wanted to make a film about Londoners and football violence, and he wanted to make a film about Londoners abroad. He's covered all that. I don't know what it will be about. *Outlaw* – it sounds like a Western. Fucking fingers crossed.'

Unfortunately, we'll still have to wait for Nick Love's take on a Western – Danny in a cowboy hat and a six-shooter would have been something to savour! But Danny could uncross his fingers, as he was indeed cast in *Outlaw* and was delighted with the results. 'With *Outlaw* he came back with a script that really says something and, after reading it, I wondered why no one else had picked up on it and made a movie about this stuff.'

The Business had steeled Love from the critics. Its success at the box office showed that people loved his films. 'The broadsheets hated *The Business* [but] for the lads mags it was the film of the year. But a lot of the British film industry hate the fact that people like me get away with it.'

And Nick Love had a novel way of obtaining funding, bypassing the British film industry and going instead to his supporters. Because of the success of *The Football Factory* and *The Business*, Love had a huge fan base – an audience who worshipped his films and, more importantly, would pay to be involved in his movie.

Instead of going the usual way of obtaining funding, they were instead offering film fans a chance to be a part of the movie-making business. Packages ranging from £10 to £100 would get them the DVD of the film, their name on the credits and a non-speaking part in the film. *The Football Factory* and *The Business* were big hits at the box office and on DVD, and for fans to be part of it was like a dream come true for the 'Big Hitters' – which they would later be called.

Love hit upon the idea after seeing a trailer for *King Kong* before the actual film had been made. He said, 'I remember thinking, If we could find a device for getting the public aware of this film before it's actually been made, what a brilliant thing that would be. So, for me, it became about wanting that publicity and planting it in people's consciousness. It also meant that we had a thousand people running around with *Outlaw* T-shirts on, publicising the film on a very underground level. Some people have since said they thought it was a very cheeky idea – and it probably was. But put yourself in my position, where you're making small films but you want them to aspire to do bigger business. To me, I work my bollocks off, so what's the point in spending all this time if only three thousand people end up going to the cinema to see it? It's so soul destroying when that happens, so you want people to know about it.'

Talking to the *Guardian* in 2007, he said, 'It seems my fan base is the DVD nation. *Outlaw* is aimed at my chav fan club. I'll put my hand up and say, "Nihilist teenage escapism was what those earlier films were about." I'm proud to be king of the chavs. Many people wouldn't be.'

Despite his claims that he was happy with his place in British cinema as king of the chavs, Love saw *Outlaw* as a chance to show the critics there was more to him than football fans beating each other up, or cockney gangsters getting a suntan. 'It's not supposed to be a full-on film about revenge and violence. For me it operates on a few different levels. A lot of men – myself included – have a fear of violence. I think a lot of men share a feeling of impotence in not being able to stand up for themselves. So that's on one, very muscular level. But the bigger issue for me is the whole social issue, where so many people feel let down by the law. I've wondered for quite a while how long it would be before people started to take the law into their own hands because they feel there's no point in calling the police. The other issue in the film was that of men facing the existential questions in life as in "What's the point? What are we all doing here?" I think that, particularly later in the film, there's a struggle to try and deal with their lives, which is why they seem to be going out in a blaze of glory.' He didn't have to look far for real-life inspiration for the film. 'In many ways it was an easy film to write because the basis for the script came from true stories and real lives. I had to make the issues slightly more extreme in some cases because, after all, it is a film. But for the most part I stayed true to the research. The kernel of it was already in existence – you pick up the papers, be they tabloid or broadsheet, and see that we are facing dark and uncertain times. Crime rates are spiralling out of control and the public generally feels helpless.'

Another source of inspiration came from the Phil Daniels character in *Goodbye Charlie Bright*. 'In my first film there was a character that served in the Falklands. I realised recently that I've got this affinity with soldiers coming home from war.' The more Love thought about it, he realised it was because of his friend's father a long time ago. 'He came home from the Falklands and slowly drank himself to death,' Love recalled. 'He walked away from his family, he just couldn't reconnect socially. I remember he worked in a scrap-metal yard and felt so overawed by the whole experience that he'd been through and yet, as far as I could tell, he was never given any way of dealing with it.'

Like Love's previous films, *Outlaw* deals with the male psyche and how men transfer their emotional problems through violence. Love said, 'Sean Bean's character is a representation of a lot of men who are drifting through their lives like ghosts, who can't connect with anybody, and feel desperate and alone. We don't live in a culture where men can easily express themselves. When he goes to see his old commanding officer, Captain Mardell, and he's asked if everything is OK at home, he says, "Yeah." He can't tell the truth – he can't say, "I'm a mess, I'm living like a vagrant in a weird hotel with this strange security guard!"'

Producer Allan Niblo was on board immediately, excited about the film's potential. On the film's production notes, he said, 'When Nick first told me about his idea for *Outlaw*, I was immediately gripped. Here was a project which tapped into the conscience of the modern audience: fear of crime and the inability of law-enforcement agencies that made us all fearful. Nick's film speaks directly to the audience, and explores their fears and uncertainties.'

Love continued, 'I remember giving Allan the first draft of the script. It was not manicured in any sense, it was a rambling two hundred pages, but it was what it was, it was the seeds of *Outlaw.* He called me two hours later and said it was a great read. The problem is, we don't feel like a community any more, we don't trust each other. The bad man has everything going in his favour these days.'

For Love, *Outlaw* was a chance to reinvent himself. And to do that he would ditch his cast of regulars and work with new and different actors. 'After making *Goodbye Charlie Bright*, *Football Factory* and *The Business*, I had to really shake myself out of what I was doing in terms of reinventing myself with a new cast and crew. It was a rebirth for me and, because I felt that *Outlaw* was a much more serious, grown-up film, it felt like it was the right time to do it.'

But, despite Nick's regulars not featuring in the film, Danny was spared the cull and snapped up the part of Gene Dekker.

As to why he kept Danny, Love reasoned, 'Out of all the actors I'd worked with in the past, he was by far the one who had the least ego and was easy to get along with. He speaks the dialogue the way it was intended to be spoken – I never had to question anything with him. But

I did think I had to make him different. I couldn't make him Frankie out of *The Business* or Tommy Johnson out of *The Football Factory*.'

Love's original plan was to cast Danny as the security-guard character – a part that eventually went to Sean Harris – until 'one day one of my partners said I was mad, that he was Gene Dekker, the easy-going, middle-of-the-road guy. Danny doesn't like violence, he's terrified of violence, he just wants to have a quiet life, which is exactly what Gene Dekker wants. So we changed his role. I spoke to Danny and, in typical style, he said, "Yeah, I'll do either. I don't care." But I think he does it really well.'

Initially, Danny wasn't that keen on the Dekker character, having not really taken any notice of him when reading the script for the first time. However, after several more reads, he realised the character's importance. '[He] was the one who was going to be in touch with the majority of the audience, he is the everyman,' explained Danny.

Danny, like Love, had grown depressed with the state of the country that he loves, saying in 2007, 'I don't think it's a very nice place to live in at the moment. Once it starts to get a bit dark, it's worrying for people walking the streets, even for me and I'm from East London. I know a lot of dodgy people in that area but I don't know anything about these youngsters that are coming up. They've got a different mentality. Gun crime was unheard of even for my generation, and I'm only twenty-nine. I knew naughty people when I was younger but none of us even thought about running with guns. Now you get fifteen-year-old kids being shot in their beds and all the American gang stuff going on. It's probably easier for these kids to buy guns than cigarettes.'

However, Danny was quick to play down any suggestions that he endorsed vigilantism. He told the *Sun* in 2007, 'The film raises the question of whether, if you had ten minutes in a room with someone who had done something horrific to you, could you actually bring yourself to hurt them? The majority of people couldn't.'

To freshen things up, Love decided to cast from a whole new pool of actors, and fantastically talented they were too. Iconic actors like Sean Bean and Bob Hoskins teamed up with talented thesps Sean Harris and Lennie James, with rising star Rupert Friend rounded off the main cast, which included Danny, of course.

Danny was clearly excited about going toe to toe with some of the biggest acting talents in the country. 'On this film I'm surrounded by actors from different backgrounds. People like Lennie James, who's been in the game a long time, and Sean Harris, who is so method in his approach. And then you've got Sean Bean, who is the A-Lister, who's done the Hollywood thing. Everyone was so good that we were all raising the game and there was a really healthy challenge between us all.'

'The first person I approached was Beano [Sean],' said Love. 'Because I had this character, this guy who was a quiet man, quite a thoughtful character but who was incredibly violent when he needed to be. The thing was I could never get Sean out of my mind while I was writing it, and the more I wrote it, the more it became apparent that Sean was right for it. Where else would you go apart from Sean? That gruff Northerner who you really believe has been out in Afghanistan. Who else? Ray Winstone? Gary Oldman? Tim Roth? There aren't that many actors of Sean's generation that you believe can be quiet and then explode when he needs to. Fortunately, he read the script and said he was in. Once you've got Sean Bean in your film, it's a lot easier to attract everyone else on board.'

Luckily for Love, Bean was excited about the script and about working with Love in particular. The only stumbling block was that Bean wasn't available for the latter half of the eight-week shoot because of conflicting schedules. But it's testament to both Love and Bean's commitment to making the film that they achieved it, as filming all the action scenes one after the other was a 'gruelling' experience.

Love recalled, 'We shot the movie in eight weeks and only had Sean Bean for four of those as he had to go straight on to another film in America. So that meant we had to shoot all the action in the first four weeks. It was gruelling but actually the sense of relief that we'd got through nearly all the hard stuff without anyone getting hurt gave us huge confidence and meant we could concentrate on the performance scenes in the latter part of the shoot. When we finally wrapped, I felt exhausted but my adrenaline was kicking in so much I was convinced I could do another couple of weeks.'

Bean didn't mind as he was determined to be involved. 'Meeting Nick got me excited about the project, his vision of the film and how he wanted to portray the character, the ideas he wanted to get across. I was so impressed by what he was trying to achieve, and I thought, This sort of thing don't come along very often, a man who's so impassioned and enthusiastic about what he wants to create. The violence comes from a deep-rooted source. It's really clear that these characters are isolated, alienated, angry and frustrated. They're disillusioned so you can see where their actions come from. That's why I was interested, and then meeting Nick and seeing that passion, that really bowled me over. I'd played a few soldiers before so I brushed up on that and observed the military side of things but there wasn't a lot of research to do. The theme of the film was all around us anyway. You only have to pick up a paper or go in a pub or talk to anybody, that's the research: it's being talked about all the time. People are very aware of it socially and politically, and I think the themes of the film are with us.'

For the part of Walter Lewis, Love was hoping to get veteran British actor Bob Hoskins. So they sent him a script and hoped for the best. Unbeknown to them, Hoskins has a novel way of deciding whether to work on a film or not.

Hoskins explained, 'My agent sent me the script and told me it was good. I read it and it passed the cold-bum test. When a script comes through my letterbox I take it to the loo and, if I'm sitting there for quite a while, I realise I've got a cold bum, then it's got to be a good script, you know? That's how I judge them.'

After the script passed Hoskins's cold-bum test, he met with Love. 'Bob and I talked about this feeling that England was not like it used to be, and feeling safe on the streets. Feeling that sense himself of "where are we going wrong?" I think Bob probably shared that anger, so it was quite easy to sign him up.'

'I met with Nick Love and I liked the way he talked about making films, and when we started I liked the way he worked,' said Hoskins. 'Drama is about private moments; it's about things that you don't normally see, emotions that people don't show. So basically the audience is a kind of voyeur looking in on something private. The way Nick shoots it, he makes the camera a sort of secret observer, and I think that's fascinating.

'As for the story of *Outlaw*, it reflects what people are saying on the streets. It's not a call to arms, it's a prophecy. Everything is weighing down on people, they're highly taxed, they're getting fined for petty reasons, they're being punished, they're being turned into statistics. The only people who seem to have any freedom in this society are criminals, and ordinary people are getting very angry. I think Nick was recording what he's seen, and it's a very strong, alarming vision of what is happening out there.'

Friend was cast as Sandy Mardell because he – as Love explained – 'was the only actor that came into the auditions who didn't play him like a crying boy'. 'It's a hard part to play,' added Love. 'He barely says a word in the whole film, but is always there, watching, feeling and, ultimately, regenerating himself through his experience. Rupert got the balance of hard and soft perfectly for the role.'

'Lennie James was always top of my list for Cedric Munroe, the barrister,' continued Love. 'Lennie has done lots of great TV work and I always admired his dignity as an actor.'

As for the part of creepy security guard Hillier, which was initially offered to Danny – that went to Sean Harris, an actor whose method approach to the role was something that Danny marvelled at.

But Love had to be convinced about Harris as he had other actors in mind. However, his regular producer Niblo kept badgering Love to check out Harris. And Love is glad that he did. 'Sean walked in and I was mesmerised,' remembered Love.

Love had his 'Outlaws'. All different actors, different styles, different personality traits – but united in making the film as special as they could.

Their first meeting, however, didn't exactly go as planned. Love decided that they should all meet up for a meal before shooting in a bid to break the ice. However, after half-an-hour of uncomfortable silence and everyone poring over the menu in a bid to keep themselves busy, Danny and Love feared the worst for the rest of the shoot. This was the pair out of their comfort zone and it looked at first as though they were out of their depth.

However, things soon went swimmingly as Danny got to grips with their particular type of acting styles. He told *Nuts* magazine, 'It's a big moment when Bob walks on set. Even though he's tiny, he's got presence. Sean's a very quiet man, a very shy man. He's quite withdrawn. I was surprised he even knew who I was, to be honest. But I did know he was excited to be working with Nick.'

Hoskins, much to Danny's disappointment, didn't bond with the actor as much as he would have liked. 'He

Above: Janet Street-Porter and Danny entertain *The New Paul O'Grady Show*.

© *Rex Features*

Below: *Straightheads'* director Dan Reed with his stars Danny and Gillian Anderson.

© *Getty Images*

At the British soap awards in May 2007, toasting Kym Ryder
and Lisa Snowdon.

© *Rex Features*

Above: Tamer Hassan, Danny and DJ Tim Westwood at the 2007 Gumball Rally.

© *Getty Images*

Below: Danny (far right) in *Severance*.

© *Rex Features*

Danny, Sean Bean and Lennie James in *Outlaw*. © *Rex Features*

Arriving at the NME awards in 2007.

© Getty Images

Danny Dyer on far right. Tea and Pinter in the 2008 production of *The Homecoming* with Kenneth Cranham (to left of Danny) and Jenny Jule.

A scene from *Dead Man Running*. *© Rex Features*

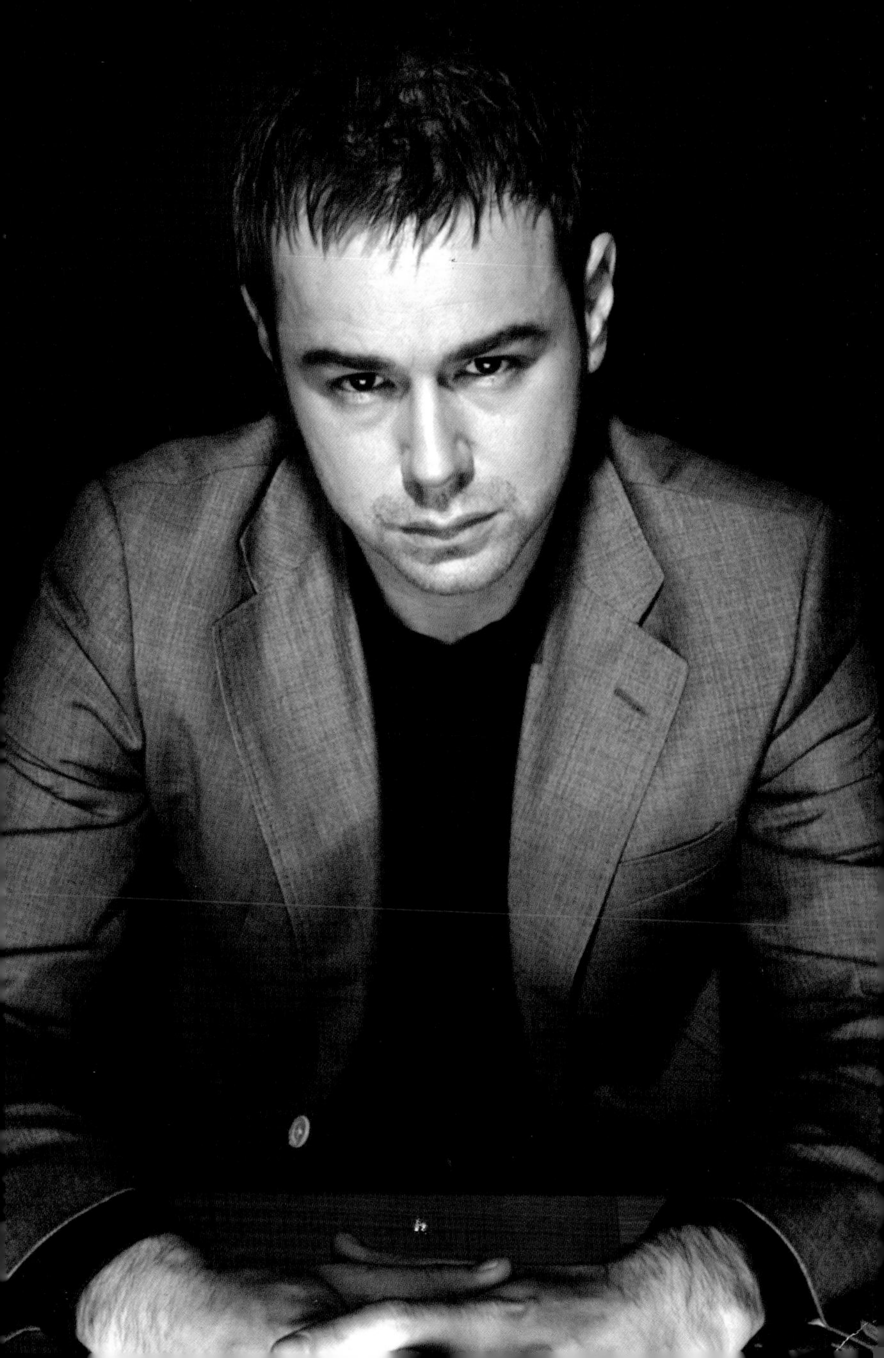

Danny in *Pimp*.

didn't get ya,' Nick said to Danny during the film's commentary track.

Danny added, 'He's Bob Hoskins. You want to fire a thousand questions at him. But you can't. One thing about Bob is he never had any fags. Bit of a ponce for his fags. It was always, "Who's got a fag?" but he's an absolute legend.'

It was during one scene with Bob that Danny knew Nick had grown as a director. 'Bob came in,' explained Danny. 'He only had a couple of scenes anyway. He did the first scene and he was rubbish, I swear to God. He couldn't get his lines out; he was all over the gaff. I sort of looked over to Nick and thought, Right, what you going to do here? But Nick, fair play to him, took him outside and told him straight. You can't fanny around with people like Bob, you've got to tell him straight, and he came back inside, sat down and he was fucking brilliant.'

If Love was going to give his film a makeover in front of the camera, he decided to have one behind the camera as well. For his three movies previous (and his short films), he had used the same crew. However, Love decided he would shake things up. And he was delighted with the results. 'I'd never worked with cinematographer Sam McCurdy before but he was amazing; such an instinct for following the emotional drama and for avoiding the obvious. His team broke all the conventions. They understood that the look and feel of the movie was just as important as the story, and worked tirelessly to make sure everything was perfect.

'Typically, the weather was against us – a real contrast

to my last film – which was shot in Spain in glorious sunshine. But Sam and I had worked out a specific look and grade for the film, which was not weather dependent, subject to the occasional bout of torrential rain. The fights and shootouts were probably the hardest to get right and look authentic. With very little time and money, you have to get them right first time, so a lot of preparation and rehearsal took place. The final shootout around the country house that carries on into the woods was shot in two days. That's not a lot of time but with rigorous planning and a great team, we sailed through it.'

Outlaw tells the story of five different characters who, for very different reasons, have become disillusioned with the state of society and feel that justice is no more in favour of the victims. These included Gene Dekker, soldier Danny Bryant (Bean), barrister Cedric Munroe (James) and student Sandy Mardell (Friend), who are recruited by hotel security guard Simon Hillier (Harris) and supplied information of future targets by policeman Walter Lewis (Hoskins).

It's a different cast and it's certainly a different look for Love. If his first film was in council estate Technicolor, *Outlaw* was set in a different England – one rooted in dark hues, heady atmosphere and accompanied with a shaking steadicam and oppressive close-ups. For his fans, used to Love's steadied colourful shots and witty one-liners, this came as a shock. But he was desperate to give his film a new look – although some might argue he was trying too hard to impress his critics.

Love, however, just believes that it is a natural growth

for him as a filmmaker. He said on the film's production notes, 'I'm getting older and I think I'm maturing as a filmmaker, and that's reflected in the film. I could have very easily made *Outlaw* in the style of *The Football Factory*. I remember when I was doing it, thinking that it was more *Mad Max* with lawless gangs running around everywhere. I think it's made in a more mature way. As I was writing it, I wasn't just thinking of the *Guardian* and the *Independent*. I was thinking of the lads who read *Nuts* and *Zoo*, and have gone out in their droves and bought the DVDs of my other films. There are moments in the film, good one-liners in the film that those sort of audiences love. So I'm slowly moving away from my roots but I'm not abandoning them completely.'

Harris, in particular, impressed Danny on set with his approach to the character. His method acting was something he and Love weren't used to on their films. 'He was absolutely fucking method,' he told *Blag*. 'He plays this racist, nutty little character so he wore his security uniform all day and then just his tracksuit later in the film.' He even went as far as not talking to Lennie James during the shooting. 'He'd say things like, "I'm not standing next to Lennie, he's black." Lenny is like forty years of age and he knows the game. After we were finished filming he was fine with it. It sets you up for a fall though, because, if you go that far into method acting, you had better be good, you had better fucking blow us away. Which he did, fair enough. A fucking great actor. It would drive you mad after a while. It would do me nut in. You would need to take a rest.'

Not that Danny himself wasn't getting bit by the method bug. Desperate to show he has a different side to himself, he turned up on set sporting a plummy English accent. Recalling the moment, Danny said to Love, 'You were like, "What the fucking hell are you doing?" I thought, Well, you know, we're trying to reinvent ourselves, the pair of us, and I was wanting to try... and you went, "Stop it, just don't do it."'

Love also recalled another priceless 'Danny Dyer going method' moment. 'I remember Danny saying he was going to go method for this. I thought, What does that mean? You going to live in a bush for six months? So he says to me, "Nah, I'm going to wear glasses." Fucking wearing a pair of spectacles makes you a method actor. I love that. If Marlon Brando knew that all it took to being a method actor was to wear a pair of spectacles, he'd have cracked it a long time ago.'

Friend, who has starred in several period dramas, admits that it was a different set to what he was used to. 'I won't lie to you; it was a very testosterone-fuelled set. The women there had balls bigger than most of the guys and gave as good as they got. But it was very enjoyable. Nick Love is probably a genius but also probably quite insane. He's an amazing guy. I look forward to seeing what he does with it.'

It was also a blast from the past for Danny, as the bullying colleague in his film was played by Paul McNeilly – an actor who Danny worked with when he was just a teenager.

'First play I ever did, Paul McNeilly gave me the part.

He was like an abusive father. Fucking great play. Dark as fuck at the White Bear Theatre – a tiny little fucking pub. And I ain't seen him since and all of a sudden Love has put him in a film opposite me, playing a bully again. Great actor, got a mad way about him.'

There were two large sub-plots that were excised from the film completely – one was a large rave scene that showed how big the Outlaws had become. But Love felt that, first, if they had really become that big, the police would have arrested them in double time, and, second, it 'felt like *The Football Factory* in a way'. The scene does show how today's working-class youngsters hero-worship the Outlaws for the way they take the law into their own hands.

Another large element excised was the attack on the media. It looked at how the media portray and twist the gang to suit their political leanings and editorial needs. 'The overriding sense of celebrity – about how the Outlaws become famous,' said Love.

Both deleted sub-plots can be seen on the DVD.

After a bright start, Danny's performance suffers in the film, not because of the quality of actors around him but because his character doesn't really have much to do but stare at everyone else and look scared. He might bookend the film as the main actor but he fades almost completely in the middle. Deleted scenes that show Dekker being bullied by his fiancée's dad gives him more back story. It would have added more to his character if they had been kept it in, as it shows he is surrounded and suffocated by bullies.

Not that Love agreed, as he was hugely impressed with Danny's performance. He said, while shooting the film, 'It's great to be working with professional actors. It's really helping Dyer. Danny's excelled himself because he's not with his usual people. He's with people who are challenging him all the time.'

Danny returned the compliment, saying, 'I've watched him grow but it works both ways, as he's watched me grow.'

With *Outlaw* in the can, Love was convinced he had made a film to silence his critics and prove that he was a director with substance. He said before the film's release, 'Without doubt, *Outlaw* is the film I'm most proud of. Not because it's necessarily a better film, but it's about something that's significant to all of us. It's about a time in this country when nearly all of us have been touched in some way by crime, or by the failure of the law. Having said that, I also like the style and the look of the film. It was a big departure from my other work stylistically and I think it works to good cinematic effect. In the edit, the idea was to grab the audience in the opening nightmare scene, and not let go of them until the final moment. I hope I've succeeded. *Outlaw* also asks more questions than my other films. As my career develops, I think more about the responsibility I have as a filmmaker, and the amazing opportunity I have to both entertain and to challenge. I hope that's the way *Outlaw* will be perceived. It's not designed as a controversial film but I do hope it gets people talking.'

Chapter Nineteen

Danny and the Sex-Files

It's just a really fucked-up love story

Straightheads would be yet another movie that would cause controversy – whether because of its vigilante content, Danny's steamy sex scenes with former 'Sexiest Woman in the World' Gillian Anderson or US *X-Files* fans wondering who the hell this Danny Dyer geezer was!

Released not long after *Outlaw*, it was bizarre that Danny would be in two films about vigilantism in such a short space of time. It looked like he was trying to be this generation's Charles Bronson!

But *Straightheads* was a different movie for Danny. His character, Adam, was a different beast to many of his other parts. As well as a change of pace for Danny, it was a huge chance for Gillian Anderson to move as far away as possible from her *X-Files* typecasting. 'I've been given quite a few scripts that had dark elements to them but most took place in the countryside with a haunted house,' she said. 'I've probably had that script six to ten times over the last ten years.'

Indeed, it was only when she was cast as Lady Deadlock in the 2005 BBC adaptation of Charles Dickens's *Bleak House* that more interesting scripts were sent her way. Speaking about *Bleak House*, she revealed, 'Because I'd been so used to being typecast, when they came to me I was literally thinking, Are you talking to me? Do you know who you are asking to do this? I felt like I could do it but I was amazed there was somebody out there who felt I might be able to do it.'

Since then, she has landed a part in *The Last King of Scotland* and then *Straightheads*. The angry revenge tale excited her. She told the *Northern Echo*, 'This is the first time a script came across my path that floored me in a way with its darkness. I'm fully aware of the presence of darkness in the world today and in my own world, the juxtaposition between dark and light – the human being-ness. That's something I always wanted to jump into. I'd wanted to express that aspect of myself and this was an opportunity to do so.

'At the beginning Alice starts out as an independent, confident, successful, professional woman. She is quite cocky and provocative, until a traumatic event stops her life in its tracks. She then becomes vulnerable, not quite sure of who she is and where she fits in the world. Then she finds an opportunity where she thinks she can right that situation, give herself peace of mind by following through with an act that takes over her life and, driven towards that end, she shows the effect traumatic events can have on human beings. You can become somebody you are not necessarily.'

Anderson was writer/director Dan Reed's first choice for the part. 'Gillian was the only actor I could ever really visualise as Alice; she captures so precisely her character's special mix of power, experience and vulnerability.'

Anderson added, in the film's production notes, 'Sometimes writer/directors can get possessive about their characters but Dan is not like that, he does not make you rigidly follow what he has written, though he is clear about who the characters are. Dan is incredibly confident and makes the whole process seem effortless, he is generous with his time and talks through things, and is completely open to things changing and shifting for the benefit of the film.'

The script came about after a particularly intense dream Reed had following his witnessing of an attempted rape in 2001. He had also developed 'intense fears and anxieties' from working on docu-dramas and violence, which he gleefully tapped into for the film.

While he had got his leading lady, he held auditions to find his leading man. It was instantly clear to both Reed and Anderson that Danny was the only person who could play Adam after impressing at the auditions.

She told *Time Out*, 'It was very clear from the minute we did readings with various actors to try and find somebody that there was chemistry, and the minute he [Danny] walked in the room it was obvious that he was perfect for the role. He's also incredibly cheeky in all aspects of himself and that just worked perfectly for the character. We had instantaneous chemistry together and, hopefully, that comes across, but you can never really tell. Those readings were taped, and clearly the producers and director feel like it was there as well. We haven't gotten into the down-and-dirty sex scenes yet. We're shooting those tomorrow so you should ask me about Danny after that!'

Indeed, the couple got on famously. As for the sex scenes, Danny was the perfect gentleman. She revealed to the *Daily Express*, 'The scene was filmed in the dead of night, with all the crew standing around with fires to keep us warm. The sides of my dress needed to be stuck to me, or it would have fallen off. I had to have two tapes on my side. But because it was so cold, the tape wasn't working and my dress kept peeling off too soon. My lover's job was to cover the tape while we were in the middle of pretending to have sex.' A tough job indeed.

Speaking before he was to shoot the graphic sex scenes with Gillian Anderson, Danny said, 'It excites me it's with Gillian as she's sexy and a great actress, and I quite fancy her. That helps but it's going to be out in the forest in the pitch black in the freezing cold, so my gut instinct is that it's just going to be really technical. And the way he [Reed] wrote it as well is really graphic, the way he wants. It's not just going to be, "Right, this is the sex scene; you'll hit it off here." He knows exactly what he wants, step by step. They are what they are, really. They're not usually sexy things to do but it's a major part of this fame. You've just got to get with it.'

He added in another interview, 'It was great. It's a

fucking weird thing to do – roll around with a bird in front of forty people. It was full-on nudity for both of us. It's about this twisted relationship where we get revenge on people. We're struggling sexually in our relationship, so playing a scene where I can't get it up is a bit weird.'

For writer/director Reed, he was delighted with the two actors he had managed to secure for his first feature. He said, 'Danny Dyer is a joy to work with, always sharp, precise, fearless and riveting to watch, and really gives it his all on the day. My lead actors are hugely experienced, intuitive professionals who have spent a long time thinking about their characters, both on their own and in discussion with me and the other cast.'

Danny fell in love with the script's dark and intriguing content immediately. He said, 'It started out appearing to be romantic, love at first sight, these two characters that just instantly click and have this amazing night, and are going to start a life together, and then it abruptly turns into a different film. Even when I got to page one hundred, I still didn't know where my character was going, which as an actor was exciting and refreshing.'

Reed was another director that Danny instantly clicked with. Dyer commented, 'Dan is a true gentleman and he makes me want to work hard for him. He knows how to deal with the film technically and also how to get us to know in our heads who our characters are without being overpowering – he is very calm and relaxed.'

For Danny, it was yet another dark film script that he fell in love with instantly. He explained, 'The darkness of it, I really love anything that's dark. Controversy is very important to me. I really like to be part of something that raises debate. Also, what really appealed to me was the love story, the twisted love story. I love the whole idea of two strangers meeting and fucking fancying each other but not really having much to say. I loved that. So you initially think it's going to be a love story but then it takes a real turn.'

Danny plays a twenty-three-year-old alarm and security-system installer called Adam – a cockney Jack-the-lad builder who is hired to do a job for Alice (Anderson). Despite Adam falling asleep on the job, she takes a shine to him. She invites him to a lavish party in the country where, after plenty of flirting, they end up having sex in the woods. 'I think I might be having the best night of my life,' he says on the drive home. However, things go horrifically wrong when, after stopping to tend a wounded deer, Danny is brutally attacked by some local thugs, while Alice is raped.

The film cuts to a month later, and Adam and Alice are now a couple. The police haven't been much use, although Alice left out the details of the rape. Adam is now impotent, spiritually and mentally. He tries to masturbate, can't, tries to have sex, can't.

Alice, meanwhile, has gone back to work and tries to get on with her life the best that she can. However, after seeing one of her rapists again by chance, she plots her revenge with Adam.

And what would a Danny Dyer film be without a little controversy? So this time, you have Anderson's character getting her revenge by putting a shotgun up the chief rapist's rectum!

Despite the controversial content matter, Danny was hugely confident of the film's chances at the box office. He said in a *Vanity Fair* interview in 2006, 'For me, it's my greatest role. People are going to be like, "Fuck!" Gillian and me absolutely clicked. I've seen a rough cut and we're dynamite on screen, I've gotta say.'

He added to the *Sun*, 'It's a real pleasure [working with Gillian]. She's a great actress, someone I can learn from, and it's really a two-hander, all about me and her. To start with, Gillian didn't have a clue who I was and I obviously knew who she was, but I think I surprised her, and she thought, He's got something about him, this kid.'

Speaking in an interview with Dan Reed, he added, 'It's probably the best job I've ever done. It's been rewarding, it being pieced together. It been tough but great. Think it's going to be a good film for me. You have to put it in, man; you just can't be lazy in this game. You can't just take the easy roles.'

As confident as Danny was, the character of Adam was one that got under his skin and, in fact, *Straightheads* was the first film set that he had worked on where he didn't pull out his roguish charm. 'I thought I was really miserable on the job but Gillian keeps on telling people I was really funny – I don't remember that, to be honest. I really thought I wasn't,' he told LOVEFiLM.com.

Being interviewed by writer/director Dan Reed, he was asked what the hardest thing about the film was. 'Being really horrible to Gillian. Not nice, man – she's a sweetheart. She weighs about six stone. She's a beautiful actress and I've been horrific to her. I don't like that. It was tough; it's hard to switch it on.'

He may not have been his usual playful self but he still taught Gillian a particular skill. 'I swear a lot normally,' she said with a laugh. 'But working with Danny exacerbated it. I mean, we all absorbed the word "cunt" into our vocabulary thanks to him. From the moment Danny and I met in the audition, we just got along really well and understood each other on some strange level. He's a joy to be with and cracks everyone up, and everyone starts swearing like him. He's made it really easy, it felt very natural.'

For Danny, his stock had never been higher. He had two films in the cinema at roughly the same time. But promoting it was taking its toll on Danny. 'It's weird having two films back to back. It's a weird one for me. Never happened before. The whole stress of promoting it, which I think is even more stressful than making it. I think it's harder. You know, I prefer getting my hands dirty, acting, trying to find the character – all that stuff's great. So I've had to come straight from *Outlaw*, which was quite a dark film, to this. That's what makes it quite hard as well, as I'm not getting a light-hearted one. You're dealing with some pretty heavy subjects. And that's taken its toll on me. I've lost a bit of personality. It's not really the time to be witty or be jokey. You're dealing with some pretty heavy subjects. It's only down to being fucking knackered, just repeating yourself, telling the same joke. It's weird.' However, he had a co-star who was all too used to the hectic and stressful pressures of media work. '[Gillian] knows what it can be like. She's had some fucking tough days. Just the whole intense fucking talking about yourself. Why you're acting. "What do you want to do next?" "What's your ideal role?" "Who's your inspiration?" All these big questions you want to answer but you need to go away and think about it. It takes its toll.'

Danny was also finding out what it was like when he stepped into geek-fan territory. He said in an interview, 'I've just met an *X-Files* geek [at a press junket with Anderson] who was absolutely in love with her. He was still shaking. I knew he couldn't wait to finish the interview so he could go home and have a wank. I could feel it. He was so like, "You're so lucky, Dan. How was it?" He really wanted to know and I had to sort of go, "Well, I'm not actually going to fucking tell you. I'm going to play it down because I know you're getting off to everything I say. You're booking it for later, son."'

One thing was clear, however: Danny was a wanted man.

'I've never been in this situation before. I'm like some sort of media whore. I'm still living in Canning Town, I've got a nice villa. It's nice. I'm getting a lot of work just now. It could end tomorrow. I've got to crack on.'

But, as tiring as promoting the film was, it's clear that Danny wouldn't have it any other way. Having to promote a film is tiring and gruelling, where the actor is stuck in a stale hotel room for a day, shaking hands and answering the same questions to an ever-revolving cast of people. It's stressful but it's all part of the job for a modern-day actor. Perhaps that's why he makes films that he is passionate about – it can't exactly be fun speaking about a film hours on end to journalists that you feel nothing about. He does concede, however, that he gets too involved with a film. He gets upset if it doesn't do well at the box office or receive glowing reviews.

'I'm proud of this film but I've learned as I've gotten older, promote the fuck out of it because I want people to see it but, now that it's out there, I've just got to forget about it. Don't ponder on it and think about what message you're sending out there. Just let it go. It doesn't belong to me now; it belongs to the paying public. Let them make up their own mind.'

Chapter Twenty

Going to America

They fucking absolutely ripped us to shreds. I've never seen no stars before. Fucking broadsheet cunts

Danny was now growing more and more confident – he had two starring roles back to back. 'I realised I'd made it when Noel Gallagher, my idol, wanted to shake my hand,' he said. 'It's been a hard slog to get here. Now I've got *Outlaw* and a film where I shag Gillian Anderson, called *Straightheads*. How fucking great is that?'

With everything looking good on the domestic front, it was time to do what every young British actor wants – to have a crack at the big time, to go toe to toe with the very best. And earn a lot of money doing so.

He told LOVEFiLM.com, 'I just want someone to trust me and take a risk with me. I'm going to go to America, do that, see what happens. I'm not that excited about it, to be honest with you. I'm going to go and do the American accent thing – I'm not going to go out as a cockney and do a Michael Caine, who'd had the rarest film career you can ever have: do a hundred and fifty films and not have to change your accent. How lucky is that? As an actor, I don't think I've proved anything yet. I want to get a job where I don't know if I can pull it off, that's what I want. I want to think to myself each day, Can I do this? Am I right for this? I want that pressure, I thrive on it'.

He had hoped that it would go better than the last time. In the early 2000s, he went to New York for a Broadway play and took a trip to LA but clearly he wasn't impressed with what he saw. 'I loved New York and loved the people,' he told the *Sun* in 2005. 'But LA is like a whole different country. I couldn't bear it. I don't want to go out there on merit. After three weeks I went, "Sod this, it's costing me too much money," and I went home. All I wanted was a Sunday roast at home in East London with the rain chucking it down outside.'

In an earlier interview in 2004, he commented, 'Maybe I just didn't have the patience, maybe I just didn't want it enough, but I hated it all. I hated the audition process, which wasn't reading for people, but was all about going out for a meal – what food you order, what sort of subjects you talk about.'

But this time he felt confident. He was a leading man now and felt he was ready to be tested against the best in the business. 'I love England, I like making British films. I'm quite into that. But listen, I want to earn a pound note like everyone else. I want to see if I can do it out there. If [Jason] Statham can do it, I feel confident.' But prophetically, he added, 'I don't know if they get me out there.'

He 'got a couple of scripts, one with Samuel L Jackson and the other one with the geezer [Zack Snyder] who did *300*, for another comic-book-strip thing [*Watchmen*]'. However, nothing materialised and he went back feeling as downhearted as the last time, when he had gone up for a part in 2002's *Red Dragon*. If successful, he would have been up against Ed Norton, Ralph Fiennes and Sir Anthony Hopkins, and directed by Brett Ratner. However, it was to be a disastrous audition process – and one that cemented his belief that he would never get a fair chance in Hollywood.

He recalled, 'I was up for a role in *Red Dragon* and they had sent me the script, I'd read it and learned it. But, when they said they would take me for a meal instead, I needn't have bothered with the script at all. During dinner I ordered salad cream and you should have seen their faces – they just looked disgusted. I don't want to say that I've ruined LA, but I just couldn't believe their reaction because I ordered something they hadn't heard of.'

Danny told another version of this story to the BBC. 'I went up for *Red Dragon*. Read the script, loved it. Learned my lines, went to the audition and I could see it in their eyes that they didn't like me. Probably because I went [cockney voice], "'Allo, mate, how you doing?" They don't get that out there. But what annoyed me is that they didn't listen to what I can do. I had to listen to their bollocks for half-an-hour and then I've just walked out thinking, What was that all about? Why am I here wasting my money?'

Whether he lost the part because of salad cream or his

cockney accent, one thing was clear – Danny felt that he wasn't getting a fair crack. He added, 'I got a bit downhearted. Wasted three weeks and wasted about five grand. I wasn't getting the opportunity. When I go back there it will be on my terms. That's where the money is and they make amazing movies, but it's not the be all and end all.'

Danny wasn't impressed with what he saw at all, adding to the *Daily Star*, 'I went out there and did a Harold Pinter play on Broadway – it was top stuff. Then I thought I'd go to LA and found out that LA's totally different to New York, and I learned that the hard way. It's all about being a celebrity out there, and they quite like the Hugh Grant, Jude Law type of Englishman. I don't fit into that mould at all. They couldn't understand a single word I was saying. Auditions out there are also totally different. You don't sit down with a script, you go out for dinner and they analyse you, what you order and shit like that. That's not me; it's not what I'm about. Give me a script and I'll fucking nail it, take me out for dinner and I'll fuck up.'

Not that Danny was having it any easier in the UK either when he got back home, because, while he was starring in two films, they weren't exactly getting five-star reviews. The *Daily Record*'s Alan Morrison wasn't shy about expressing his disgust for *Straightheads*, giving it a one-star rating and labelling it a 'nasty, vindictive, badly scripted, violent fantasy that plumbs new depths when our heroes kill one guy by sticking a rusty shotgun where the sun don't shine'. He wasn't too complimentary about

Danny either, saying it was 'the worst performance of the year in the worst film of the year – a British vigilante film that's even more offensive than *Outlaw*'.

However, *Straightheads* was given an easier ride than *Outlaw*. The critics' fire was aimed more at Love's film than Reed's (which did also attract some glowing reviews, to be fair).

Outlaw was savaged by a majority of critics, earning a twenty-five per cent rating on review accumulator site Rotten Tomatoes. The *Mirror* called it ugly and simplistic – film critic Ali Catterall stated that it was '*Death Wish* meets the *Daily Mail*', while *Empire* magazine said it was the 'kind of film the tabloids will call to ban. Don't take that as a reason to see it.'

However, *Variety* praised the film, saying, 'Both the pic's power and its problems stem from Love deliberately taking no moral position, nor offering any solutions; he gives his audience what it wants at a gut level and doesn't wimp out at the end. Coming from a director who's always distanced himself from the Brit filmmaking establishment, it's a pic by an outsider about outsiders. Simply, in that respect, it's a bracing, if hardly likeable, accomplishment.' The reviewer also hailed the acting. 'Thesps grow in their roles as the story proceeds, with Bean very believable as the disillusioned paratrooper; ditto the always interesting Dyer, a Love regular, as a conflicted everyman. In an initially supporting role, Hoskins comes into his own with a powerful speech at the halfway mark.'

Variety aside, the reviews put paid to Love's earlier

prediction before the film came out. 'I would imagine *Outlaw* is going to have a bit of an easier ride because it's not wall-to-wall violence. I think it speaks to more people. It's got a much wider target audience, it's not catering to one particular demographic, there are different characters in different walks of life. There is a lot more to latch on to in *Outlaw* than any other film.'

Love was stunned by the reaction. When he came to record his commentary track for the film, it was plain to see how hurt he was by the reviews. 'I wasn't expecting it to be so hostile. Bottom line is this film got a fucking hostile reception when it came out – a lot of the press didn't like it. Thought it was too violent – thought it was glorifying violence. You know, the maddest thing is they thought this was a country that didn't exist. The press was saying, "How can you say we live in a lawless country?" and there are nonces running around and people running around stabbing each other. What fucking paper are you reading, you dozy cunts?'

For Danny, the reception was too much – getting to the point that he has now stopped reading reviews. 'I gotta stop doing it. It's not healthy. Fucking getting wound up by critics. It's fucking terrible. I have started getting knocked by the critics and I'm not used to that. I'm used to people loving me and what I've done. They are saying that I'm doing a lot of the same stuff. I know it's just the critics but I know that I haven't proved myself as an actor. I have maybe showed twenty per cent of what I can do.'

Love was unrepentant, however. He told Danny, 'These films take a while. Like *The Business* – they cunted that, calling it "lazy filmmaking" and [saying that] the acting was bad. *Time Out* cunted the life out of it when it came out. It was on the telly the other day and they listed it as film of the week. The cinema is not the be all and end all. That's just fucking vanity. This will be the most important film we've done in our lives. In years to come when they do a retrospective of your life, they'll be saying *Outlaw* was the most important film you did.'

Chapter Twenty-One

A New Stage in Danny's Life

It's about learning your craft again

With Danny's film career taking a bit of a hit, he decided to tread the boards – something that he has done repeatedly over the years. Danny may be seen as the hardman geezer in lad films but he is, in fact, a respected actor on stage as well.

It's all thanks to Nobel Prize-winning playwright Harold Pinter. Hailed by many as the generation's most influential playwright, his plays were regularly seized on by Danny, who took Pinter's striking word play (with one critic calling him the first white rapper) with ease.

Pinter was, in turn, incredibly fond of Danny. Veteran stage and screen actor Kenneth Cranham revealed that Pinter treasured a Danny Dyer comment. He said, 'When Michael Attenborough directed us all in *The Homecoming*, he mounted a picture of the cast and we all wrote things on the back. Danny Dyer wrote, "Harold, you're the bollocks." Harold said it was the best thing anyone had ever said about him.'

Danny starred in the run of Harold Pinter's *The Homecoming* from January to March 2008. The play, which had been running since 1965, deals with an all-male household in North London. It explores the reaction of the family when they welcome the homecoming of their eldest son and his wife. Danny plays Joey, with Jenny Jules, Neil Dudgeon, Nigel Lindsay and Anthony O'Donnell also starring.

Attenborough picked the cast because they all 'have a feel for Harold's work'. 'Though I can say it myself, it's beautifully cast,' he joked to officiallondontheatre.co.uk.

It was a part that had an adverse effect on Danny's home life. He explained, 'My missus never takes any notice of the jobs I'm doing. I like that. She's old school. When I come home there's dinner on the table. Never asks about anything. The other day she said to me, "What's this play about?" I said, "Why?" "You've been acting funny" "OK, I'll tell you what the play is – I play a rapist." "Oh, I thought so," she said. "What do you mean, you fucking thought so?!" "You've just got this mad way about you, looking at me funny." And I thought, am I? Am I looking at you funny? I have been a bit fucking off. But that's only because it's about not snapping out of character. It's about living and breathing it. You've got to because, once you walk out on that fucking stage, I can't have any doubt in my mind, so you do sometimes take that home with you. Obviously I'm sitting indoors eating my dinner like a rapist, fucking dribble all over my face, looking at her arse! It freaked me out a bit.'

The play was, in fact, a real homecoming for Danny, who hadn't trod the boards in years. It gave him a buzz to be back, a chance 'to get back to your roots. It's about learning your craft again.'

As it was his first play since he'd struck it big with films like *The Football Factory* and *The Business*, it was a chance for his fans to see him in a completely different media. They came in droves. A journalist was stunned to see a load of Danny's fans pile in. In fact, one audience member was so stunned to see her favourite actor that she couldn't stop telling her friend next to her about it during the play's first act. Unsurprisingly, she was escorted out.

The journalist, who didn't want to be named, revealed, 'It was chaos. The word had obviously got out on Danny's internet forums that he was in the play and it was like a bus had arrived from Chav land! I managed to speak to one of the actors, who said it had been like that the whole run, and that Danny attracted all this unwanted attention from his film fans that couldn't sit through a two-hour play.'

Danny, however, was glad to be able to attract a brand-new audience to the theatre, saying that he got 'a lot of my mob in. It's good to get the young birds back in the theatre. Not being a theatre guy myself, it's always a surprise to see so many people show up. I'm happy.'

So were the critics, with curtainup.com saying, 'The cast are near flawless in their portraits of two-dimensional anti-heroes. In particular, Kenneth Cranham's foul-mouthed paterfamilias Max is an excellent study of a warped alpha male. Nigel Lindsay is the suave, articulate and intensely menacing Lenny and portrays a strange mixture of superficial charm with an undertone of absolute charmlessness. Danny Dyer is the taciturn, vain Joey with unfulfilled aspirations to be a boxer, and Neil Dudgeon gives a first-rate performance as Teddy, the most civilised and successful son, who is also the only one with the sense to escape.'

'Pinter's black comedy remains pretty much as sharp, sleek and shocking as ever – and it is beautifully executed here, in Michael Attenborough's excellent production,' said the *Financial Times*.

The *Observer* raved, 'Nigel Lindsay's Lenny is first rate too. He is full of false bonhomie and veiled hysteria. Like his father, he is a random raconteur. And as Joey, Danny Dyer does not miss a comic trick, even – or especially – when steeped in catatonic reverie.'

Danny performed in another Pinter play, called *Celebration*, which was first put on as a double bill with *The Room*, also by Pinter, in early 2000 at the Almeida Theatre in London. *Celebration* focuses on three couples dining out at an expensive restaurant and the existential musings of the restaurateur, played by Thomas Wheatley.

Danny played the waiter, and it's his stirring speech that closes the play. *The Spectator* wrote, 'At the end of the evening it is the young waiter (Danny Dyer) in what should be an award-winning performance, left alone on stage to confront his own demons, who has not only the last words but also the most immediate claim to our ultimate attention.'

The other Harold Pinter play that Danny featured in was *No Man's Land*. A play that was first written in 1974, it tells the tale of a rich alcoholic writer who drunkenly invites a stranger to his house, where the stranger tells him that they knew each other at university. His menservants Briggs and Foster are sceptical of the stranger's motives.

In 2001, the Nobel Prize-winning playwright directed the play at the National Theatre, which saw Danny playing Foster, alongside John Wood, Colin Redgrave, John Wood and Andy de la Tour.

Though the *Observer* called Danny's performance flat, the *Independent* hailed the production, calling it a 'brilliant revival' and 'unforgettable'.

Sans Pinter, a young Danny played a gay man in Peter Gill's 1999 play *Certain Young Men*. While the play received mixed reviews, there was one person in particular who was wowed by Danny's performance – openly gay pop star Boy George. The singer was convinced that Danny was gay in real life. Danny explains, 'He saw the play and he really thought I was gay. He was on my fucking case. I was like, "Listen, man, I think you're the bollocks, but I'm not gay." He just wouldn't accept it. He was at an awards ceremony and I shit my pants. He's a big man; he's an aggressive man. I was standing up against him and the curtain, and he sort of pushed me, and I fell back on to my arse and I had to go home after that. I was flirting with him a bit. I was playing with him but he wouldn't accept the fact I wasn't gay.'

However, Boy George was hurt by Danny's comments and Danny has since apologised, as mentioned in a previous chapter.

While Danny has proved to be a hit on the stage, the reason he hasn't trod the boards on a more regular basis is down to two reasons – the first one being money.

He told *The Student Pocket Guide*, while working on *The Homecoming*, 'You get some actors who do theatre constantly. They're very respected and very good actors but they're skint. I know I'm in the game, which I love, but I want to earn a pound note out of it. It's been seven years since I done it. Thought I needed to do it again for the kick up the arse but it's been crippling me. I get a buzz out of film and I get a buzz out of theatre but you can't live on it. Four hundred quid a week. I know it sounds like I'm some greedy cunt over here but for four hundred I've got to give fifteen per cent to my agent. I was picking up about three and a half. That's beer money.'

The other reason he favours film over the stage is that he gets bored of playing the same character. Speaking before the end of his work on *The Homecoming*, he said, 'I've got one week left of the show and I'll be honest with you. I've had enough. I struggle with saying the same thing every night, to be honest.'

Chapter Twenty-Two

Danny on the Telly

TV writers are so precious about their two-bit dialogue

Danny's relationship with the small screen is a complex one. For starters, it not only gave him his first taste for acting but it also gave him an important apprenticeship in small roles in some of the biggest British shows. As the years have gone on, however, he has viewed the small screen with some resentment. 'I've sort of tried my best to stay away from TV,' he told the *Yorkshire Evening Post*. 'I like making movies. I don't like the restriction of TV, the watershed, that there are only certain subjects that you can tackle. It hacks me off a bit.'

In fact, he only did his appearance on *Mr & Mrs* for ITV after having been hit by a 'naughty tax bill'. 'I didn't think I would ever go down that route. A weird experience because it's something I don't really want to do.'

Adding to that, he told the BBC, 'I've used everything

I've learned from all these amazing actors I've worked with. I'm still in a position where I don't pick and choose my roles. Nick's the only one who writes for me. All I can do is do what's put in front of me. I'm lucky that some great things have been put in front of me but a lot of it has been absolutely rubbish. The key is to make sure you shine in it – so people say, "Oh, that was rubbish but he was good in it." That's all you can do. I can't turn down roles; whatever is put in front of me, I'll do it. I did *Rose and Maloney*. Never seen it before in my life but I will do it. Sarah Lancashire's great in that, as is Phil Davis, but after these films it's not what I want to be doing. TV is so restricting; writers are so precious about their two-bit dialogue. I love the freedom of film.'

Despite being constantly linked to *EastEnders*, Danny said, 'Being on a soap for sixteen years would be my worst nightmare – like Ian Beale or Ken Barlow, who've been in the same role all those years. I don't understand how you can play those roles for the same time, but then I do understand that they have a nice house and a family – they've got their security. I ideally want to try something new but, having said that, I'll probably end up working in *EastEnders* now, won't I?'

He has since gone back on his words and, when asked where he would like to be in ten years' time, he says now, 'I want to be healthier, want to work when I want to work, be in *EastEnders*. That would be my dream.'

Despite his reluctance, Danny has impressed in recent years when he has moved over to the small screen.

Danny joined a host of famous actors who played the adult parts in hugely popular show *Skins*. Despite the youngsters being then largely unknown cast members, the adults were played by well-known British actors, including Danny, Harry Enfield and Arabella Weir.

'It's like the old *Tom & Jerry* cartoon where you only ever see their legs,' explained Channel 4's senior commissioning editor for drama, Francis Hopkinson, when asked why the adults only appear on the periphery.

Danny plays the young stepdad of Michelle – who clearly resents her new stepfather: whether it's for sponging off her mother (Weir) for cash for his latest harebrained venture, or for eating his cornflakes too loud. Despite the short time he is in the show, he makes a meaningful impact.

Before *Skins*, he had a memorable appearance in an episode of the second series of British show *Hotel Babylon*. In it, Danny plays a star premiership footballer who is staying at the hotel in preparation for a quarter-final clash again a non-league football team. But Danny's character Dave Osbourne, the captain of the team, has no plans to have an early night in. The episode features Osbourne engaging in a cocaine-fuelled romp with girls and snorting the drugs off the buttocks of a beautiful girl. The show also features former *EastEnders* star Chris Parker and *Little Britain*'s David Walliams.

He then signed up for *Kiss of Death* – a two-parter British detective thriller more in the mould of *CSI* than *The Bill*. Originally called *Blood Rush*, the script sees Louise Lombard head up a special crime unit of policemen, forensics and profilers in a bid to catch a serial killer.

Despite his initial reluctance that the show 'would dig out familiar faces like [*The Bill* actress] Claire Goose' for his co-stars, he was excited about getting the part nonetheless. However, he feared he might be made to look like a fool at the audition after not quite understanding the script – which was a non-linear story told from different perspectives from the police to the murderer himself.

'I read the script the night before and I didn't have a clue what it was about. I thought, If they're going to start asking me all sorts of philosophical questions in the audition, I'm screwed.'

Danny needn't have worried, as he was hired by director Paul Unwin straight after the audition. Danny plays Matt Costello – a laddish right hand to Kay Rousseu (Lombard). Danny was also relieved to have a great cast to work alongside, including a chance to team up with his old *Human Traffic* co-star Shaun Parkes.

For Danny, however, this was a chance to shed his hooligan image, telling whatsontv.co.uk, 'It wasn't necessarily about the script the first time. It was just about someone considering me to play a detective, which I never really get to play. Usually I'm a villain, the other side of the law. And so I was quite chuffed someone would even think of me to play a detective. When I'm getting asked on the street, "What are you up to next?" "Oh, I'm playing a detective," they're like, "Oh, what?" They're a bit disappointed in that. A bit of a mixed reaction really. But I don't work for the fans, I work for myself and I want to try different things.'

Despite being created by *Waking the Dead*'s Barbara Machin, the one-off drama wasn't commissioned for a series – which was something the producers obviously hoped for, but not necessarily Danny. 'I need to make a decision if I want to be tied down to a series. It's great to be a copper but if you sign on the dotted line I could be tied to this series for another six years. Do I really want to be tied to that? I don't know.'

But the novel idea of showing the same scene over and over again from a different perspective was a turn-off for a number of TV critics. 'Massively confusing,' said the *Scotsman*. It was a reaction that obviously would have disappointed Machin as she felt the disjointed narrative would have made it stand out among the many detective programmes in TV land. She explained the show to the *Sun*. 'There's always more than one perspective to a crime. In fact, every point of view tells a different story. So this approach allows viewers to get under the skin of all our characters – to be right at the heart of the action, and see the story from the most compelling and exciting perspective at any given time. And each time you think you finally understand the truth, hopefully, immediately afterwards we will take you somewhere new.'

However strong his apparent distaste for TV, Danny has become almost a household name thanks to his TV-hosting work. In *The Real Football Factories* Danny heads back to the genre of football hooligans – and he visits football-hooligan firms from Yorkshire, Scotland, the Midlands, Lancashire, North West England and London. The series was produced by Bravo, and Jonathan Webb, programming director of the company, was delighted to have Danny on board. 'As a big fan of *The Football Factory*, I want to pay homage to Nick Love's film with *The Real Football Factories* and am delighted that Danny had agreed to be our frontman'.

Danny had mixed feelings about the show because he didn't want to be accused of glamorising hooliganism – but at the same time he freely admits to doing the show for the money. 'Some of these people wanted to go on camera because they knew me from my acting and I had to play up to that. Some would see the TV camera and just wanted to be famous for all the wrong reasons, as if being violent was something to be proud of. This ended up being guerrilla filming and it's really hard to explain but, when I was offered it, as a jobbing actor, you just don't turn work down. I ended up having to just walk around and talk to hooligans.'

However, the shows and subsequent film work meant that Danny was in a situation he was not used to. 'I'm very happy. I've got a child on the way, movies coming out and I'm doing this documentary coming out about football hooligans. I'm comfortable and it worries me because I worry that something will go wrong. I like being the underdog, being against it,' he told the *Guardian*. 'I like to struggle. I prefer to be skint than have a bit of money. I like to be in an uphill battle. At the moment I'm on an even playing field. It's good but it worries me.'

However, there were more things to worry about while filming the show, particularly a trip far removed from his comfort zone of London. One of the episodes of *The Real Football Factories* had Danny travelling to Scotland to sample the unique taste of an Old Firm game. When interviewing Rangers fans in a pub full of angry supporters following a Celtic win, he started thinking long and hard as to whether this was the right show to be a part of.

He told the *Daily Record*, 'I didn't feel very safe. I was there with the cameraman, who weighs about six stone, and a girl from the production company with a clipboard. If I had known how terrifying making this programme would be, I'm pretty sure I would have said no. It may look like I'm being made welcome but that was far from the case. These people took me under their wing but then some weren't happy and I even got kicked while I was in a pub and I had to leave. I'll tell you one thing; I'm not going back to Scotland any time soon.'

Sheffield proved to be a tough location as well. When he went to meet the Sheffield Wednesday hooligans, he stood outside their local pub, worried about what a group of hooligans would think about the London actor who was playing a hardman. He heard the chants from the pub growing louder and louder. Fearing the worst, he walked into the pub.

The show's assistant producer Miranda Heck recounts the rest of the tale. 'He needn't have worried as he was greeted by a pub bursting with hooligans chanting,

"There's only one Danny Dyer." They were full of admiration and respect for Danny, perhaps feeling they could relate to him through his character in *The Football Factory*, and told him stories of violent incidents they'd been involved in over the years. As people they were interesting, kind and often intelligent. I was surprised by how hospitable and genuine most of the subjects were. Most held down jobs working in factories or as labourers or running their own taxi firms.'

Following the show's success, and despite the fears of last time around, Danny was signed up to do a follow-up – *The Real Football Factories International*. This time Danny would meet up with some of the most notorious football gangs in the world, including Brazil, Poland, Holland and Italy.

If he thought the experiences making the first one were a tad hair raising, he was to get an almighty shock once he left Britain. As he says in his foreword in *The Real Football Factories* book by Dominic Hutton, 'We were a small crew – me, a producer, a director and a researcher. We were shot at, stoned, chased and tear gassed. We were threatened, challenged, offered out and we weren't always sure we were going to come back in one piece.

'We ran for our lives in Holland and we just escaped a glassing at Galatasaray. And while travelling to a game with a Brazilian firm we came under gunfire from rival fans and had the windows of our bus shot out.'

There was a certain bravado from Danny there, as he wasn't actually there during the shooting in Brazil but the rest of his team was. He had to head to London for work but told the team, 'Stay lucky, yeah?' Prophetic words indeed.

He revealed to the *Sun*, 'In Brazil the director and film crew were on a bus with hooligan fans of Sao Paulo's Palmeiras club and they came under gunfire from rival supporters of Botafogo. A car chased the bus and the crew had to crouch on the floor to avoid being shot, and I was glad I wasn't with them. That's how serious they take football there. It was like a movie script.'

But there were some hairy incidents nonetheless. And some of them didn't have to be so physical. He recalled to the *Guardian*, 'The thing that freaked me out the most from doing this football documentary was the whole raping thing. In Serbia they like to rape the other firm. They get the head guy, rape him and send him back. That freaked me out. They don't want to bash him; they just want to fuck him up the arse. The ultimate power. I didn't expect shit like that. I thought it'd be real right-wing, macho-type guys. They were adamant they weren't gay but... c'mon!'

There was an upside, however, as the experience has made Danny a far more cultural person. He explained to the *Independent*, 'When I was filming *Real Football Factories International* I visited nine countries in two months. Through that, I learned that you really have to embrace different cultures when you're abroad. Britain is so multi-cultural but you still get those Brits-abroad types who search for a fry-up. People miss out if they're too set in their ways. I really enjoyed meeting lots of different people and trying different food.'

He would be meeting different people yet again, when he went on to present a brand-new series of *Danny Dyer's Deadliest Men* for Bravo. He has go on to do three series at the time of writing.

Bravo controller Dave Clarke hailed his signing of Danny Dyer, saying, 'His down-to-earth delivery and inquisitive nature gives us a unique angle on some dark characters that our audience will likely be intrigued, shocked and surprised by in equal measure.'

Like before, his reasons for doing the show were financially motivated. 'I'll be straight with you. I've got a mortgage. The offer came when I needed a bit of dough as I've just bought a five-bed place in Essex. I've hit thirty-one and started to get a bit sensible about money, building for my kids' futures. I'm trying to get them out of the ghetto because I'm still living in Canning Town.'

Also, in the *Mirror* interview in 2008, he admitted that films are 'my passion and what I'm about. But films, especially British ones, are few and far between and I'm the only breadwinner in the house. It's not a nice decision to make, putting yourself in mad situations with dangerous characters. Or good for your health.'

Or even good for publicity. The show had its fair share of controversy, including a media storm in Belfast when Danny posed for a picture with former loyalist Johnny 'Mad Dog' Adair and convicted terrorist Sam 'Skelly' McCrory.

Adair, not helping matters, told the *Belfast Telegraph*, 'Like his film *The Business*, Danny is the business. He's such a cool guy. Why are people worried about me meeting him? I met him because he was doing some documentary work with Skelly and I was asked to contribute to it. I'm not telling people where the photograph was taken or if we had any drinks together, but we got on fine. Johnny Adair is still a name for the documentary makers and I'm not going to apologise for this. My old enemies are just jealous of me meeting people like Danny Dyer.'

It was headlines like those that forced journalist Janet Street Porter to launch a withering rant at the show, saying in her column in the *Independent*, 'Danny is a decent actor who's even appeared in Pinter plays, but this enterprise is shameful. The whole mess is laced with unnecessary shots of guns pointing directly at the camera.'

Controversy aside, the regular images of Danny strutting in front of the cameras, sneaking fearful glances to the viewers and doing the faux hardman act, were causing him enough problems as it was. His hardman-geezer shtick was wearing thin for some people. Revered and reviled in equal measure for the tag, it wasn't long after the shows that Danny was to get something a celebrity fears the most – their very own spoof alter ego.

Terry Alderton's short sketches on Virgin Media as 'Danny Dire' have made him extremely popular on file-sharing sites like YouTube, and his catchphrase 'proper fucking naughty' has been frequently shouted at Danny when he is making his public appearances in nightclubs with his pal Hassan.

It was never Alderton's idea to spoof Danny. It all

happened three years ago when Alderton was hosting a celebrity auction event in Essex. He claims he was doing some 'gentle piss-taking' on the celebs that turned up, including Danny and Hassan. Two years later Alderton was asked to do some interviews for Virgin Media for the V Festival. 'I was getting quite annoyed because it's not my thing. And I end up seeing Tamer and Danny, and I go over to them to do an interview. And Danny's like, "You took the piss out of me two years ago." And he's a bit, you know, giving me some aggro and then he just walks off. Tamer looks at me and shrugs his shoulders, and shakes my hand and leaves – and I'm holding the microphone myself in front of the camera. Anyway, the next day I was flicking through the TV and I saw him on *The Real Football Factories*, and I just thought, I could do something here.'

Since then, Danny Dire's popularity has soared, despite it being a very short-lived series of skits. 'People do parodies of my parody on YouTube.'

However, he admits he feels guilty for the embarrassment caused after he met Tamer again at an event. 'So Tamer looked over at me, laughing but wagging his finger. So I walk over to him in my Danny Dire walk, and he's still laughing and wagging his finger at me. I go up to him and he goes, "You've ruined him, you've ruined his self-esteem. You've mockneyfied him." I didn't mean to ruin him. Tamer asked me if I did it because of the V Festival thing and I said it started after that, and he was like, "I fucking knew it. I told him it was a big mistake, that you would make him pay." But you know what? He did it to himself with those shows. People come up to me and say, "He's just a London boy, a cockney geezer like me." And I'm like, "You're putting it on, mate. No one is like that in London." What's even funnier was when he was with his missus on *Mr & Mrs*. She was worse than him! Fucking hilarious. I was like, "Is she for fucking real?"'

Of course, it doesn't help that Hassan constantly jokes about it to Danny. 'I think it's hilarious,' said Tamer, laughing.

'Oh, it is funny but he's, he's, he's ... all right,' admitted Danny begrudgingly. 'That fucking Terry Alderton.'

No matter how much it is mocked, it's clear from watching the first episodes of *The Real Football Factories* and *Danny Dyer's Deadliest Men* how much Danny has grown as a presenter. Some may feel he still has flaws but he is far more confident, has toned down the geezer banter and has become one of the most distinctive faces and voices on British TV.

In recent years he has played down the hardman angle, saying in the *Independent*, 'I come from East London and am quite open, the way I speak. People assume I'm a hardman, which I'm not. Dyer the tough guy – I hate it. I'd rather be known as a sensitive soul.'

He felt it was time to get away from his previous roles. 'I feel I haven't proved myself as an actor at all. I've done the leading-man bit but I haven't been stretched. I'd like to play something I can get my teeth into and play against type. It's a vicious circle because I'm quite well known now and I get scripts for drug dealers, lunatics and cheeky chappies. I'm trying to break away from that a bit. Maybe do period drama – tights and all that. I draw the line at fucking Shakespeare though!'

Chapter Twenty-Three

Danny the
Family Man

*I'm going to be running round with a baseball bat,
looking for men who have upset my daughters*

One thing the TV shows did was provide some stability in his life. An actor's life can fluctuate from really busy to penniless. And with Danny becoming a dad for the second time in 2007, it was time for him to be responsible. Sunnie was welcomed into the family by a loving father, mother and an inquisitive sister. 'Dani's very excited about it,' he explained in a 2007 interview. 'She's got her insecurities as well, like, "Am I still going to be your favourite?" But that's natural. I'm sure she's going to take to it naturally, like we will as parents. In a couple of years I'll have her babysitting.'

When asked if he would live his life differently, he tellingly revealed, 'I don't think I'd do anything different. Maybe I'd have a kid a bit later in life, but then I like the idea of Dani being twelve and I'm only thirty-one, so when she's eighteen I'll only be thirty-seven. Everything happens for a reason. I believe in fate, so I wouldn't change anything. I'm really embracing being a dad second time round.'

Danny was a teenager when he had a child for the first time and he freely admits that he had understandable worries as to whether he could do it, whether he was grown up enough and whether he could be responsible. He showed that he was by going back to labouring in a bid to support his child during the early days.

'I became a dad at nineteen and there's nothing like having a kid to make you get out there and bring home the bacon,' he explained. 'I did some pretty lousy jobs just to pay my way, but that made me really determined to make it in the movie business.'

After not being there fully, he cherishes his second chance with her. 'I totally adore Dani and it's so great to be taking her to school, bringing her back and actually being a dad again. Instead of seeing her every Sunday for a couple of hours, which is what I was doing before,' he told the *Mirror* in 2003.

'Last time I had a kid I was useless. I was nineteen and didn't know what I was doing. This time around I'm really embracing it: it's given me a real drive in self-belief. She's the bollocks; she made me grow up a bit. The feeling you have for this thing that you've created and watching it grow. It's a weird thing to explain. The whole first year just flies past so quickly when they are learning to walk and hold that bottle up, just little moments and the first words out of their mouth.'

The reason he did *Outlaw* was for his kids. 'It's not just the guns,' he told the *Sun* in 2007. 'It's that we live in a society where paedophiles are grabbing kids out of parks and there's no deterrent. What frightens a paedophile? They get eighteen months on a segregated wing, which is kushti for them. If you're going to give them eighteen months, put them in a normal wing. Then it feels like eighteen years! I'm the father of a ten-year-old girl and I'm frightened to let her out every day. I can't not do it just because there's a very small chance she'll be snatched off the streets and used for someone's sexual gratification. That fucking frustrates me. It makes me angry.'

While he has become more responsible than ever, there is one thing that he can't control, no matter what, and he dreads the day when it will happen – when his daughters eventually start dating.

'I think my daughter has got the worst two combinations. She has got the beauty and scatterness. She's scatty and she's beautiful. I know she's going to cause me a lot of aggro.'

He told *Now* magazine, 'It changes your outlook on life. And having two girls frightens the life out of me. My forties is going to be a stressful decade. I'm going to be running round with a baseball bat, looking for men who have upset my daughters.'

Talking to *Film Review* in 2005, he added, 'It's very important that I've got a good relationship with her. I couldn't think of anything better than being a dad. It really grounds me and makes me feel special.'

And it's clear that Dani is a daddy's girl, enjoying an incredibly close relationship with her dad. 'She is the apple of my eye. She is also very interested in what I do.

Dani knows what I am auditioning for and we sit and watch my films together. Mind you, I have to tell her when a naughty bit is coming and she will cover her eyes.' Which is probably why he wants to make 'a bit of Disney or something' in the future for his kids.

While she watches films with her dad, she gives him a quick steer when she has any homework queries. 'I'm not an intellect. That's not my game, spelling and all that. I can't spell, bless my little one. I can't help her with her homework. She's now got to the point that she blanks me. If she's got a problem, she won't ask me. She'll ask the dog.'

Despite his love for his children, he has admitted that two may be enough for him for the future. 'I am thinking about the snip. Only through the lack of sleep, because you get ratty around your missus. But there's nothing better than watching your old women give life.'

He admits that it's Joanne that has made him a great and happy father – because she is the love of his life. Talking to AskMen.com, he said, 'As long as you're loved up and soulmates with the person you have them with, you'll be fine. It's the biggest expression of love you can possibly give to someone and, if you're not with the right person, it's going to be a fucking nightmare.'

However, he admits being nervous about the birth of Sunnie, as he hoped he and Joanne would handle it differently. Talking to the *Observer* in 2007, he admitted, 'First of all, the baby brings you and the missus together, then after a couple of months you can't stand each other and you start rowing, and you're covered in sick and shit.

I'm hoping this time we're not going to go down that route, but it's hard work.'

Of course, having Danny as your dad must have its moments. For a large section of working-class Britain he is a national treasure and it's something that 'fascinates' his young daughter. If she ever decided to get into acting, Danny would encourage it.

'There are a lot of bitter people out there who have got jobs that they hate and the key to life for me is doing something you love doing. Take your own path. As long as she is happy in what she does, I'll support her in whatever she wants to do... as long as it isn't lap dancing.'

Chapter Twenty-Four

The Future's not Dyer for Danny

I'd love to have a crack at Dr Who

While he worked with Parkes on *Kiss of Death*, Danny also worked with another *Human Traffic* familiar face a year previously – the film's director Justin Kerrigan was on helming duties for the 2007 music video for the song 'Two Lovers' by The Twang. Starring Danny and Ray Winstone's daughter Jaime, it's a highly stylised tale of a romance between two recklessly in love youngsters.

Kerrigan told XFM, 'I wanted the film to be a story of a modern Sid and Nancy couple but drawing heavily on *Mean Streets* and *Nil by Mouth*. I wanted a contrast between the gritty environment that the characters live in and the tenderness of their relationship. We brought Danny Dyer to do what he does best, and that is be Danny Dyer. This allowed him to totally act the boy, which is where Danny shines. We always knew that the band were going to be in it – they are great performers on stage and we thought that the perfect role for them was to play Danny's mates in the pub. We had no argument from them when we said that they would have to have a few drinks as part of their role.'

And, despite his presence on the small screen, Danny was still a film star first and foremost.

He had a brief cameo in Noel Clarke's *Adulthood* – the sequel to *Kidulthood*. Like the first instalment, it's a gritty, hard and moving look at life in the inner city of London. Danny appears briefly as a boyfriend of Claire – one of the characters from the first film.

'When I read it I couldn't understand some of the dialogue, the way these youngsters speak. I like what Noel Clarke has done and thought I'd give him a bit of support,' Danny said.

The role came about through his friendship with Noel Clarke on the horror comedy *Dog House* by *Evil Aliens* director Jake West, who said in 2007, 'I think this will be my best movie to date. It certainly has one of the best original scripts I've read in years.'

Danny, Clarke and Stephen Graham star as a group of men going through a mid-life crisis, who end up taking a weekend trip after Danny has his heart broken after a painful divorce. They end up in a town full of beautiful women. Problems arise when they discover that the women have become insane from an airborne toxin and want to feast on the flesh of men. To defeat the 'zombirds', they arm themselves with remote-control cars, golf balls and water pistols filled with nitro fluid.

Writer Daniel Schaffer said, 'The women, rather than being mindless zombies, are all personifications of our heroes' paranoias and fears of emasculation. Of course, this is all in the classic zombie action movie with loads of blood and gore.'

Clarke was adamant to say that it was nothing like *Lesbian Vampire Killers*, a project that Danny was once attached to. 'It's comedy horror and we've seen a few of those before. There are parallels in the respect that the women are the killers but it's a completely different film. It's a lot more laddy. I don't know if you can call them [James Corden and Matthew Horne] lads. They're just two comedians who are very funny but this is Danny Dyer, Stephen Graham and me, and it's more laddy.'

Danny himself was excited about the film's chances. He said, 'It's a movie I've got really high hopes for. I've got an opportunity to work with someone I've always liked and respected – a Scouse actor called Stephen Graham who was in *This Is England* and *Snatch*. Great actor, someone I've known for a long time but never got to work with. I've just got really high hopes for it. It's like *Shaun of the Dead*.'

Danny also appeared in the farce *The All Together*. It told the story of Chris (*The Office*'s Martin Freeman) who is both frustrated with his career as a TV producer for a rubbish prank show and his odd flatmate. Things get complicated when he gets back from an eventful day filming and finds, because of one plot contrivance after another, a gangster, a corpse, his flatmate, a clown and a group of estate agents in his living room.

Danny played one of the gangsters who gets killed. While the film suffered terrible reviews, Danny does show again some nice comic elements as a gangster wannabe who is suitably impressed with his American counterpart (played by Corey Johnson). 'I didn't really know where to go with it because the dialogue has him as a real villain. But I thought it would be better to play him trying to be a gangster, getting it wrong.'

Indeed, it seemed Danny's part was the one that most people remembered. The film's writer/director Gavin Claxton told Danny during the film's commentary track, 'People come up to me amazed. I didn't think you could do that.' To which Danny replied, 'I've been getting that as well. I love comedy. I've done comedy before. I'm sick of dark films, man. I want a bit of light-heartedness.'

Danny was originally up for the part of the annoying TV presenter Jerry Davies – which would have been a great cast-against-type part for Danny. Claxton was impressed by Danny's audition but when Richard Harrington came in he was torn between the two. But he didn't want to lose Danny so he offered him the part of Dennis.

Again Danny (and Freeman) weren't paid big bucks for the film. 'The reason I decided to do this film was because of the script. It was definitely not the money that attracted me. All the main actors were paid six hundred quid a week. This is the Equity minimum wage,' said Freeman at the premiere.

Danny added, 'I'm just taking the piss out of myself. It's not really like my other films.'

Next up was *City Rats*, which reunited him with Tamer Hassan – on the credits, at least, as the pair don't actually share a scene together.

Directed by Steve Kelly and written by Simon Fantauzzo, the film, which has been described as '21 *Grams* in London', tells the story of eight strangers who have lost their way in life. Danny plays Pete, a former drug user who helps a mother find one of his old friends who has gone missing. They begin a journey to find her lost son. It's a gritty tale that shows depth and intensity from Danny. For his female fans the film may be something of a shock – out goes the trim, handsome Danny in place of a plump, unshaven and sweaty alcoholic, although, as his character says, 'Alcoholics go to meetings, I'm a drunk.'

It's a highly stylised film with Danny and Hassan impressing in their segments, particularly Hassan. It's bound to be a must-have for Danny Dyer fans and shows why he is held in such high esteem by them.

While Danny has said he wants to make some films for his kids, perhaps they shouldn't watch the latest version of children's fantasy tale *Alice in Wonderland* by Lewis Carroll. *Malice in Wonderland* is a gritty, gangster-set reimagining of the classic kids tale. Starring *Lost*'s Maggie Grace in the title role, the film, which has been described as '*Alice in Wonderland* meets *Lock Stock and Two Smoking Barrels*', tells the tale of Alice meeting some larger-than-life characters after suffering an accident.

Danny plays the enigmatic taxi driver Whitey. The film's director, Simon Fellows, enthused about the film, saying, 'It will have a terrific pace and energy with a sound and editing style that will push contemporary interpretation to the cinematic limits.'

Producer Carola Ash said about the film, '*Malice in*

Wonderland takes its inspiration from the internationally loved story *Alice's Adventures in Wonderland*, and is the wildest, most contemporary interpretation yet. *Malice* is a rites-of-passage road movie with the sexiest female lead since *Tomb Raider*. Aimed firmly at a global audience, *Malice* will tap into, and build on to, an already extensive awareness of the Lewis Carroll classic, bringing a fresh new perspective to those familiar with the story and an exciting thrill-filled adventure for others.

'All the characters from the book are there,' she added, 'but their names have been changed to present day. Like, for example, the White Rabbit is Whitey, and he is a hip drug dealer. There will be surreal elements, as opposed to fantasy. The film will be dark. It does have its thriller moments. It's gangland UK but it's all good fun too.'

It seemed it was good fun off camera as well. Former club bouncer and now boxer Earl Ling plays a henchman called Two Guns Tony. However, his training exercise for his next fight was thrown into chaos because of Danny. He explained, 'He's just a down-to-earth lad. I spent a great deal of time with him and went out drinking with him in Yarmouth last August. I had to take a week off training after spending three nights out with him!'

While it stars Maggie Grace, the role was originally due to be played by *The OC*'s Mischa Barton and, before that, oddly enough, Kelly Osbourne.

Danny said about the film, 'I play the white rabbit, and its really mad and stylised. Maggie Grace plays Alice. She was in *Lost* and in *Taken* so she's quite hot at the moment, so it was great to work with her.'

He was also lined up to star alongside rapper 50 Cent in *Dead Man Running*, 'It's about one guy who basically gets in a serious bit of trouble with a real gangster and he's got one day to live or he's going to get ironed out if he doesn't raise the funds. So, it's basically about a dead man running, which is him, and I play his sidekick, who's trying to get him out of trouble,' explained Danny.

While you couldn't think of a more unlikely couple than 50 Cent and Danny Dyer, Danny couldn't wait to work with the rapper. 'I don't know about him as an actor. He's definitely a presence. We come from totally different backgrounds but he's a great artist. It's going to be insane.' The film would also see him reunited on the big screen with Hassan for the first time since *The Business*. 'It's great to work with Tamer again.'

However, while Danny was teaming up with Hassan again, he was saying goodbye to Nick Love. For now, at least. 'Nick Love's doing another film, called *The Firm*, using unknown actors,' said Danny. 'It's a shame but our paths are going in a different direction.'

Produced by Vertigo Films, *The Firm* is a remake of the 1980s football-hooligan film. Love said, 'The original *Firm* was the sole reason I became a filmmaker. For me, the pull of the casual culture wasn't so much the violence, it was the music, the clothes, the clubs and girls, the swagger and confidence everyone embodied, that's how I see my version of the movie.'

And for someone so strongly linked to London's East End, it shouldn't come as a surprise to find that Danny was linked to a part in *EastEnders*, despite his earlier reluctance. A source for the show told the *Sun* in March 2009, 'Danny is ideal for *EastEnders*. He's actually from the East End – and still lives there – and he's got the whole geezer thing going on.'

But a BBC spokesperson added, 'It's very early days. No role has been offered to him.'

Danny told *New* magazine in April, 'I love the show and, yeah, we have had a few meetings. Ideally, I'd love to play against type and not always be the hardman – but it's all down to casting and how they see you really.'

He even hinted that he might fancy a little ride in the Tardis. 'I'd love to have a crack at *Dr Who*. I think I can do something mad with it. Just instinctively, I know I can do something with it.'

Maybe the thought of doing TV finally appealed to Danny. And therein lies his contradictory nature. He's the loud-mouthed gossip hound who hates the nature of celebrity; he's the easy-going, likeable chap who is incredibly analytical about his work and passionate about making the films that he wants; and he's the hardman, swaggering geezer who treads the boards, does naked cover shoots and has a played a number of sensitive characters.

His heart remained in his birth town. His former schoolmate Julianna Sandy said, 'A number of people from both my year group and Danny's did not do much with themselves after school. Many of them had kids, did not continue with their education – so it's good to see someone succeed, and publicly, so that others can see that you can make something of yourself regardless of your background. It's not often that someone from the East End that is normal makes it big.'

No other actor has been so entwined with a city. 'I love London and I'm a Londoner through and through, and proud of it,' he says. A burden it may be at times but it has also made him who he is and he, or his fans, wouldn't have it any other way.

Chapter Twenty-Five

A Difficult Year for Danny

Things had been looking incredibly bright for Danny. Film roles were coming thick and fast, he had signed on to write a weekly column for a lad's magazine while he was keeping out of the limelight – with his mouth set on 'No controversy'. However, it's fair to say that Danny hasn't had an easy time of it despite his best intentions.

First up – *Malice in Wonderland*.

Despite the presence of Dyer and Maggie Grace, the movie came and went without any real fuss. A shame, then, as it's probably his most interesting performance in years – with *Guardian* critic Peter Bradshaw (not one normally keen to rave about a Danny Dyer film) commenting, 'Dyer has some funny lines, and he makes the most of them, proving that he is actually a good performer, all too often marooned in endless geezer knees-ups.'

The Times as well noted that it was an 'amiable central turn from Danny Dyer'. Despite Danny's assured performance, the film was otherwise rated as below average from many reviewers.

Doghouse was given a bigger release around that time, no doubt due to the film riding on the crest of the horror comedy craze. Director Jake West certainly milks the film's central joke of the British lads versus the zombies and Danny clearly has a ball playing the loveable rogue. So critics spent most of their effort on the movie criticising the fact that it was just the latest in a long line of blokey horror-comedy films – a theme that was in danger of being overdone thanks to films like *Lesbian Vampire Killers* and *Shaun of the Dead*. Again, the majority of the reviews were unkind – with *The Guardian* accusing it of 'Undeniable misogyny' and 'creative bankruptcy'.

Pimp was given a limited theatrical release – and was savaged by critics. 'With nil insight – into the sex industry or anything else,' wrote one, 'you might conclude *Pimp* is a film for men who get their kicks watching Dyer strut around leering at topless women.'

Talking at the world premiere for the film, Dyer himself said, 'I'm not gonna say I get bored of playing the gangster types – but I worry about people seeing me in the same kind of roles again and again. It's something that people like to see me do and I do enjoy it but I'm ready for a new challenge.' He conceded that his gangster image made him a sex symbol, adding, 'The things they [female fans] send are really disgusting, filthy, terrible. They even disgust me and I'm a tough guy to disgust.'

Danny teamed up with Sean Bean for thriller *Age of Heroes*. 'I play a WWII commando – it's an old-school action flick, with me running around ironing out Nazis, I can't wait,' he said. 'Thing is, they're sending me up to Scotland to put me through my paces first. The bloke I'm going with is a major, so he won't fuck about ... It's going to be hard work, but I want to make a proper go of this film.'

But work was interrupted on the film due to illness and a cloud of volcanic ash from an Icelandic eruption which trapped them in Norway. Danny told *Zoo* magazine, 'I'm suffering badly because of all this shit. I'm filming this WWII movie with Sean Bean and we're in a fucking bad way up here – and because of two acts of God, we might not even be able to finish this film. The first one is the lack of flights because of that bloody volcano. But the second is a virus that has spread through the whole crew. Everyone's dropping ill, people are spewing up left, right and centre... It's a nightmare. I've swerved it so far, but we can't fly people in to replace the ones who've got it. We're just stuck up this fucking mountain, waiting to get sick. It's totally surreal.'

Back home, *Celebrity Big Brother* offered a reported £200,000 for the actor to appear in the series – but he wasn't interested, reasoning, 'There was no way I was doing it. It's not worth the aggro. Plus, by the time I'd paid my bills, I'd only have seen half the cash! It would purely be a money-making move, but you risk screwing up your career.'

But the small screen was an ever-present fixture for Danny, with the actor starring in extra-terrestrial documentary *I Believe* – a TV show which saw him investigate whether there is alien life on earth. And it seemed while Danny was working on the show, he got a bit too close to the story – telling journalists, 'I saw one, yeah. People think I'm a complete lunatic now but I did see something a bit mad. I went to America, to a hippie commune and had to get a bit spiritual... I went to meet some people who have been abducted and things like that and they told me some really mad things. I think you have got to open your mind a little bit. I just want to believe that there are things out there. I did see something. It wasn't a plane, it wasn't a helicopter; it just looked like a massive star going across the sky. But it freaked me right out.'

His column continued to be a great source of comfort for his fans – getting their weekly Danny Dyer fix. However, he was to find himself in the middle of a storm once more as a result of it. He was asked for his advice on how to get over a break-up and said that the ensuing controversial words attributed to him were 'completely misquoted' – while the magazine blamed it on a 'regrettable production error'. The actor told *The Sun*, 'I am totally devastated. This is not the advice I would give any member of the public' Dyer's column came to an end not long after. The idea of him as an agony aunt, as ironic as it was supposed to be, had always been likely to raise eyebrows.

His attention was turned elsewhere when he was devastated after thieves broke into his house in the middle of the night in November 2009. The first he heard of it was when Joanne woke him up in the morning, shaking. It was there he discovered that thieves entered his Essex home while everyone was sleeping and stole his Porsche and Mercedes. While the cars were later found by police just miles from his house ('I'm lazy and I didn't fill it up so they probably panicked and just dumped it'), he was more concerned about comforting his daughters – who were justifiably shaken up by what happened.

But Danny has always known how to bounce back. It's been something that has been constant throughout his life – just when he's at his lowest he seems to grapple his way back to the top. Last time it was Nick Love who jolted Danny's career back to life, and he could once again breathe new life into his film career.

Arguably, Danny's biggest film was *The Business* and it's been heavily rumoured that it's a world he'll return again. Set in the '90s, it will explore a look at the ecstasy drug trade during the acid house era. Whether that transpires or not, Danny will continue to take risks and latch onto promising directors with talent (Love, Andrea Arnold and Christopher Smith for example) in a bid to ensure he stays one of Britain's brighter talents. His life has been one full of ups and downs, and it looks set to continue down that path. But we guess he wouldn't have it any other way.